Sailing Through LIFE

Life Lessons for Young Adults

Sailing Through LIFE

Life Lessons for Young Adults

Varun Wadhwa

Anecdote
Publishing House
For the love of quality reading!

Anecdote
Publishing House
For the love of quality reading!

anecdotepublishinghouse.com
champreaders.com

Anecdote Publishing House
2nd Floor 2/15 Lane no. 2 Ansari Road,
Daryaganj-110002

Published by Anecdote Publishing House
Copyright © Varun Wadhwa

First Edition 2024

ISBN 978-81-973806-3-1

MRP ₹ 399

All Rights Reserved.
No part of this publication may be reproduced, stored in a retrieval system, or transmitted in any form, or by any means — electronic, mechanical, photocopying, recording or otherwise — without the prior permission of the publisher. Opinions expressed in it are the author's own. The publisher is in no way responsible for these.

Book Promoted and Marketed by Champ Readers Pvt. Ltd.
Edited by Meraki
Cover Design by Rishikumar Thakur
Layout by Graphic Tailor
Printed by Thomson Press (India) Ltd, New Delhi

For the heart of my heart, my six-year-old daughter Inayatt Someday, when you look for inspiration and life lessons, I hope you pick up this book

CONTENTS

Foreword		ix
Prologue		xiii
Introduction		xvii
Chapter 1	Because Confusion is a Bliss	1
Chapter 2	Problems are Obligatory, Suffering is Optional	11
Chapter 3	Learning the Fundamentals of Learning	19
Chapter 4	The Relationship & Network Conundrum	30
Chapter 5	Priority Number One: Health	40
Chapter 6	Financial Literacy & Money Consciousness	49
Chapter 7	Have you Read the User Guide of this Mind?	57
Chapter 8	Failure is a Virtue	66
Chapter 9	Spirituality is for Everyone	75
Chapter 10	Don't be Shy to Seek help: Speak Up	83
Chapter 11	Hidden Key to Success: Involvement	91

Chapter 12	Trade Your Best Friends for Books	98
Chapter 13	Create a Social Media Brand for Yourself	108
Chapter 14	Reserve the Complains & Criticism for Yourself	116
Chapter 15	Because Givers Always Win in the End	124
Chapter 16	Do not Romanticize with the Romance	132
Chapter 17	Productivity Hacks: Master Them	138
Chapter 18	Expression of Joy vs Pursuit of Happiness	148
Chapter 19	Respect Your Mortality	153
Chapter 20	The Most Important Thing	163

Epilogue	*169*
After Thoughts	*173*
Acknowledgments	*175*
Notes	*177*

FOREWORD

I feel honored to share about this wonderful book written by my dear friend Varun Wadhwa. I have fondly seen him grow by leaps and bounds, as a professional pursuing his passion as a public speaker and an author besides his corporate career.

His belief in himself is something that will make you his die-hard fan and the result is another masterpiece written about youth.

More than 40% of India's 1.4 billion people are under 25: a massive, tech-savvy, and mostly English-speaking labor force, with their eyes set on the future.

I feel if there is a revolution that can come in the nation, only youth has the power to accelerate it.

My youth friends, today one of the biggest reasons for anyone's career growth is awareness of digitization, technology, and automation. But sadly, due to excess digital consumption loneliness has started prevailing more. I notice how excess screen time has affected the lives of youth, both in positive and negative ways. And this is where I want the youth to understand life. The majority of youth has stopped seeing and feeling the world with their own naked eyes. That's where the real inspiration is, that's where the real innovation is, that's where the real inclination should be.

Here is what I suggest—pause often. Observe the intricate patterns—the dew-kissed spiderwebs; the sun-kissed leaves, the laughter lines etched on a loved one's face. Life's beauty lies not only in grand vistas but also in the tiniest stitches. Seek wonder in everyday moments—the aroma of freshly baked bread, the touch of a friend's hand, the way sunlight dances on water. These are the golden threads that illuminate your tapestry.

Life's tapestry will bear scars—a tear here, a faded hue there. These are the moments when you'll need to mend. Gather resilience, compassion, and self-love. Stitch them into the frayed edges. Let vulnerability be your needle, and authenticity your thread. Remember, it's okay to unravel sometimes; it's in the mending that strength blossoms.

Sailing through life is an inspired, heartwarming, motivational writing that cannot be read with your eyes but can be experienced in the sanctuary of your soul.

In my opinion *Sailing through life* is a classic book that allows the youth to expand awareness and live from a place of compassion, clarity, passion, resilience, and universal love for all humanity.

Get ready to be rescued from the stressful uncertainty and fear-driven environment that's increasing unnecessary chaos, drug abuse, and stress, and enter into the world of inspiration through the experiences shared by the author in the book which will uplift you spiritually and mentally.

The book reiterates and teaches you the immeasurable quality of tenacity, love, and acceptance of life within the realm of understanding the power of being you.

The loom of life invites you to dream audaciously. Imagine

a world where your passions collide with purpose. Picture yourself scaling mountains, both literally and metaphorically. Dream of starlit nights, when your aspirations shimmer like constellations. And then, my dear reader, take that first step. For dreams, when pursued with tenacity, become the warp that holds your tapestry together.

As you turn these pages, remember that you are both a weaver and a storyteller. Your choices, experiences, and heartaches—they all contribute to the grand narrative. So, my young friend, weave boldly. Use vibrant threads of curiosity, resilience, and love. Create a masterpiece that reflects your essence—a tapestry that whispers to generations yet unborn.

I appreciate Varun for his research work touching the real human challenges through his personal touch of writing. Thank you for sharing your gift with me and the world and most of all I cherish you. God bless the day you were born.

My reality of youth life is all about—resilience, motivation, humility, and getting up every time I fall.

I am no public speaking expert. I am an expert public speaking student, that's my story and I am sticking to it.

To your success,
Author Sherry
Recognized by the Prime Minister of India.
Founder & Chairman – Institute of Professional Speaking
Founder & CEO - MS Talks - A public speaking platform given to more than 60,000 public speakers worldwide and trained over 2,00,00 individuals across 23+countries
International Public Speaking Coach, Mentor, Global Professional Speaker, 11 times International TEDx Speaker, 4 times Josh Talks Speaker, Author of International Best Sellers, Authored 10 books.

PROLOGUE

The old man sat on a weathered wooden bench, its paint faded and chipped over the years. The river flowed gently before him, its waters reflecting the soft hues of the setting sun. The air was filled with the soothing sounds of flowing water, birdsong, and the rustle of leaves from nearby trees.

His wrinkled hands rested on his lap, weathered and worn like the bench beneath him. Deep lines etched across his face told tales of a life well-lived but also carried the weight of regrets. His eyes, clouded with time, gazed into the distance, lost in the currents of his memories. A soft breeze carried the scent of earth and dampness as if nature was whispering to him. The old man's gaze shifted from the flowing river to the horizon as though seeking answers in the vast expanse of the world. His mind wandered back to moments long gone, and a sigh escaped his lips, heavy with the weight of unfulfilled dreams.

In the distance, the sun dipped below the horizon, casting a warm, golden glow over the landscape. The old man's thoughts were like the curving river, flowing through the bends of his past, each turn revealing missed opportunities and choices left unexplored. Regret clung to him like a shadow, and he grappled with the echoes of what could have been.

The rhythmic babble of the river seemed to mirror the rhythm of his thoughts, a steady reminder of the passage of time. As the light faded, the old man remained seated, contemplating the course of his life. The evening draped the scene, capturing the old man's reflections of a lifetime filled with defeats and the haunting specter of unrealized dreams.

The man stepped forward to touch the flowing river as he saw his reflection in the water; suddenly, his memories flashed back as he remembered coming to this place often as a child playing alongside his friends. Suddenly, his heart was gripped with bemusement and regret; he saw himself trembling with fear and anxiety. The old man stepped back not because his life was ending but because he wondered if his life could have taken a different turn had he paid attention to his inner calling. As a young man, his eyes were filled with dreams of a bright future filled with ecstasy and fulfillment. But the labor of trying to feed a family and to build a house had taken away those dreams, like the stream of river swallowing the peak of floating wood.

He thought about his beautiful wife, who stood with him throughout his struggles, always encouraging him to pursue his dreams and never complaining about the house's lack of resources. He also thought about his two children, who were now married and lived away with their families.

He realized his stubbornness and reluctance to change prevented him from reaching his full potential. He wished he had been more open-minded and willing to embrace new ideas and opportunities. But it was too late now. Sitting alone on that bench, the old man couldn't shake the feeling that he had wasted his life. He had spent so much time clinging to the past that he missed the chance to grow and evolve. And now, as he faced the end of his journey, all he could do was rue the opportunities he had let slip away.

Soon enough, the sun had drowned in the mountains, the breeze had stopped, and the birds had settled in their nests. It was a moment of absolute silence. The old man thought about his life and couldn't help but think that life is always teaching us something new, something meaningful, something that could alter our lives forever, only if we stop for a moment and care to pay attention—the kind of attention it deserves.

INTRODUCTION

During my teens and early on in my twenties, if someone had told me that not too long from now, the world would explode into a plethora of information systems, network streams, and unlimited career options, I would have outrightly rejected the idea. But you look at the world now, and all you can see is that the young ones today have options everywhere in terms of what they would like to learn, from whom they would like to know, what career to choose, or even make an alternative career path that no-one has ever explored in the past. In short, the world has become crazy!

Today, there are enough sources of information available to young adults on the internet; in fact, the problem is that there is just too much information, and it becomes challenging to separate the wheat from the chaff. Therefore, when I thought about how this book should look, what it should talk about, and how the audience should perceive it, the only thing that came to my mind was simplicity.

In a world where people have made a profession of making simple things complicated and claiming that it is intelligence personified, we need more platforms where people make complex things simple. The real sign of intelligence is when

I can explain a black hole to my six-year-old daughter and get her all excited about discovering it when she grows up *(well, not as enthusiastic as she is to read about the beaches of the world, but close enough)*. Intelligence is also when she asks you about the reason why we pray to God, you do not tell her just to shut up and pray. Instead, you try to explain to her about the creator and the creation so that she feels more curious and prays with more fervor *(the simpler word is passion)*. As a teacher, intelligence is explaining to a student why he needs to study so that they do not make an enemy out of you. As a mother, intelligence is introducing your daughter to the concept of having to go through the menstrual cycle without making her feel shameful or degraded about it.

In short, intelligence is sophistication wrapped up in a veil of simplicity. It's not just what we communicate but also the way we communicate. Therefore, I've tried to present some ideas and opportunities in a way that's easy to comprehend and implement in your life. These learnings are like a little explosive device; if you absorb them and point them in the right direction, they will create the most mesmerizing fireworks.

The book is also wrapped up with some stories and experiences of real people making their mark in this world. I hope these stories will inspire you and help you better understand the topic and how it can impact your life. During the entire course of this book, I have not tried to impose any of these ideas upon the readers; these are merely impressions from the various experiences that I have gone through in my life alongside the decade-long research that I have done on the subject. The research is a culmination of reading and re-reading over a thousand books from various domains, meeting some of the most learned speakers, consultants, and authors across the globe, and simply observing life in general.

Why Read this Book?

If you want to become rich, this book is for you. If you want to become healthy, this book is for you. If you want to become more creative, this book is for you. If you want to become wise, this book is for you. If you want to become successful, this book is for you. I don't claim any of the above stuff, sorry. Please don't leave me here, wait.

If you want to read this book for any of the above reasons, please take my advice and donate it to someone else. If you are one of those people who doesn't believe in donating stuff, then exchange it for books that offer you the opportunity to become rich or successful.

The only reason that I want you to read this book is because someday you will realize that what I have learned is something that should have come to me a long time ago. You see, there is always one of the two pains that everyone needs to go through in life: the pain of discipline or the pain of regret. The pain of discipline may be tedious, but once it starts showing results, it becomes sweet. However, the pain of regret is hurtful, cruel, and, unfortunately, permanent. Therefore, I would not like you to regret that these learnings came too late when you lost your zeal to live. And, of course, with these learnings, you can become healthy, wealthy, and wise, but there are no guarantees. The real secret lies in eating the apple, not studying its composition.

We must understand, life is a specific combination of time and energy; while time is constant for everyone, we can play around with our energies. These learnings will fill your life with the energy you need to aspire, plan, and live a bigger life. People would look at you and ask how you are doing this. When that happens, you walk away planning your next conquest, not with a sense of arrogance but with pride. And when you have conquered enough, someday you will take stock of your life. Hopefully, you will pick up the correct measuring scale. If you pick up the measuring scale of money, you will do grave injustice to yourself. The accurate measure of a beautiful life is in terms of how many lives you touched upon during your lifetime, in the sense of what difference you made to make these lives better in some manner. And if you have become successful in that measurement scale, do me a favor. Would you raise a toast to yourself, look towards the heavens, and thank God for this beautiful gift called life? There's no need to finish the entire bottle!

How to Read This Book?

Pick up any chapter you like; they are equally good or bad; remember, simplicity is my best friend. However, the best advice that I have received on approaching any concept is never to believe what is being told blindly but, at the same time, never dismiss a subject as entirely frivolous. Allow the advice to sync in, perform your research, play around with the subject, brainstorm over the ideas, and then finally apply what you think is right for you. Use it if it works for you; otherwise, throw it away for good, but give it enough time.

So, if you want to read this book in a bar with loud music, be my guest, but I would advise you to read it relaxing around the swimming pool or beach instead. I only favor water reading because sometimes you must escape the world to involve yourself deeply into the subject. I know you are thinking, who reads a book in a bar, you idiot? OK, I take back my words; the point is to read where you can reflect on what's written. Otherwise, my thousands of hours of researching and writing time would go for a toss, fine hundreds of hours. In the book *Deep Work*, Professor Cal Newport explains that 'Deep Work' is focused on undistracted work, which is how to thrive in today's information economy. His method of blocking off chunks of time to focus intensely on a single task strengthens our ability to learn complex things quickly and optimize our output, a critical skill for knowledge workers and those who work with information.

If you observe, you will notice that half a dozen things are usually all it takes to change your life for good. If these twenty learnings are too much for you to absorb, perhaps start with half a dozen that you connect with the most. Think of these learnings as tools of transformation, growth, enlightenment, and saving time.

You can thank me later. Start chipping away!

CHAPTER 1

BECAUSE CONFUSION IS A BLISS

WHEN NARENDRA (Swami Vivekananda's birth name) first met Sri Ramakrishna, he was a skeptical young man, questioning the existence of God and the validity of spiritual experiences. However, his encounter with Sri Ramakrishna changed his perspective forever. Sri Ramakrishna, a deeply realized spiritual master, recognized Narendra's potential and saw beyond his doubts. He patiently nurtured Narendra's intellect and guided him toward spiritual exploration and self-discovery.

Despite his initial reservations, Narendra was deeply drawn to Sri Ramakrishna's teachings and began to spend more time in his company. He engaged in philosophical debates, asked probing questions, and sought clarification on various spiritual concepts.

One day, Sri Ramakrishna took Narendra to the rooftop of a house and asked him to look at the sky. As they gazed at the vast expanse above them, Sri Ramakrishna suddenly placed his foot on Narendra's chest and exclaimed, "See, my child, how you feel!" At that moment, Narendra experienced a profound ecstasy and spiritual awakening.

This incident had a profound impact on Narendra. It shattered his intellectual skepticism and opened his heart to the reality of spiritual experience. He realized that actual knowledge cannot be acquired through mere intellectual analysis but must be directly experienced.

From that moment on, Narendra dedicated himself wholeheartedly to pursuing spiritual knowledge and self-realization. He became a devoted disciple of Sri Ramakrishna and immersed himself in intense spiritual practices and contemplation.

Narendra's transformation into Swami Vivekananda is a testament to the power of lifelong learning and the importance of being open to new experiences and perspectives. His journey from skepticism to spiritual enlightenment underscores the transformative potential of education and the continuous quest for knowledge. Swami Vivekananda's life inspires us to remain curious, humble, and committed to the pursuit of truth, both in the external world and within ourselves.

If there is one thing that I wish were to happen to you, it is that you never conclude anything. It's a strange but great way of looking at everything. If you are confused about confusion, wait.

Confusion is a natural human emotion that we all experience occasionally. It can be caused by various things, such as new information, conflicting ideas, or simply trying to make sense of a complex situation, like finding a gift for your partner. While confusion may be uncomfortable, it can also be a sign of growth and learning, so instead of visiting Archies Gallery, if you ask her best friend for advice, congratulations, you have learned. But you see, a person who is confused is often the one who does not believe in anything; that person wants to seek the ultimate truth, and that person wants to look at everything just the way it is. Now, let's reverse our life clock and think of a time when we were searching for a solution or an answer to a question, and the first thing that we read or heard from someone became our ultimate truth. Maybe it was an opinion disguised as a fact, just like the below examples:

i. "Chocolate ice cream is the best flavor."
ii. "Everyone knows that early risers are more successful."
iii. "The new policy is terrible because it will ruin the economy."
iv. "That movie is objectively bad because it didn't win any awards."
v. "I can't believe you like pineapple on pizza; it's disgusting."
vi. "It's a fact that immigrants are responsible for all the crime in our city."
vii. "Studies have proven that people who wear glasses are smarter."

Vishen Lakhiani, in his book *The Code of Extraordinary Mind*, mentions that:

What if everything we think about how the world works—our ideas of love, education, spirituality, work, and happiness—is based on Brules (bullsh*t rules) passed from generation to generation and extended past their expiration date?

- "You have to become a doctor/lawyer/engineer to be successful."
- "Girls shouldn't play with trucks/action figures; they should play with dolls, and the opposite for the boys."
- "You're not good at sports, so you shouldn't try."
- "Money is the most important measure of success in life."
- "Being popular is the most important thing."
- "You have to act tough and never show your emotions."

- "You have to follow the crowd and do what everyone else is doing."
- "Success means having a high-paying job and many material possessions."
- "People from different races/ethnicities/backgrounds are inferior/superior."
- "Failure is unacceptable and should be avoided at all costs."
- "Your grades determine your intelligence and future success."
- "You have to go to college to have a good life."
- "Creativity and art are less important than academic subjects."
- "You must always follow the rules without questioning them."

The next time you are confused about a subject, don't go too hard on yourself; it's a good sign. It can lead to deeper understanding. When we are confused, we are forced to think more deeply about a topic or situation. In that sense, we become more open to new ideas, perspectives, opportunities, and possibilities. We can reimagine our world and become even more creative by using our existing resources more efficiently. Sometimes, though we may be confused because we are dumb, that's not a good thing; read enough books so your dumbness washes away; more on that later.

But if you are not in the dumb category, let's move to a virtuous circle of confusion and growth.

We would notice that confusion can lead to greater possibilities because it breeds curiosity; which leads to our minds becoming more open to new ideas and thought patterns. We can then use this to expand our learnings and gain wisdom. Just be mindful that when we grow, let that growth be a stimulus to

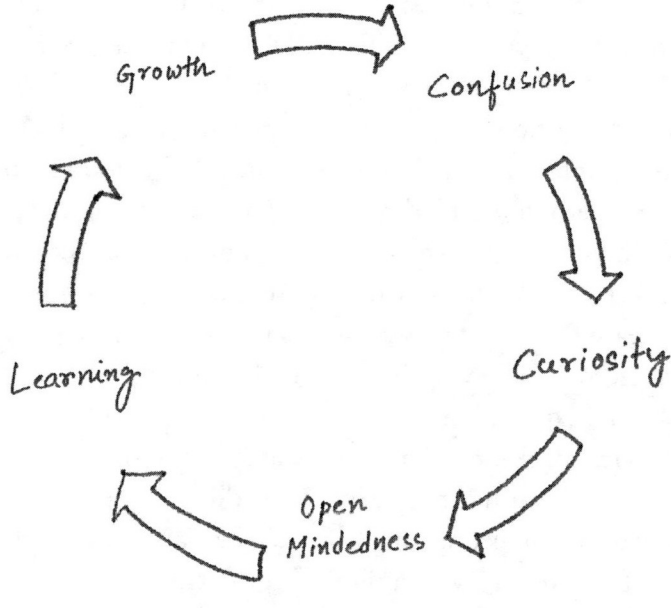

Figure 1: Virtuous Circle of Confusion and Growth

further confusion; it means that when we grow, remember what triggered this growth, the fact that we never accepted anything without seeking the ultimate truth.

Sir Isaac Newton, the renowned physicist and mathematician, is credited with discovering the Law of Universal Gravitation. According to legend, the story goes that Newton was sitting in his garden one day, pondering the mysteries of the universe, when an apple fell from a tree and hit him on the head. Maybe he was sleeping; who knows? All we know is this event sparked Newton's curiosity. He wondered why the apple fell straight to the ground rather than floating or flying away. We also don't know if he ate that apple, but that's irrelevant. The important thing is that seemingly simple observations led Newton to delve deeper into the nature of gravity and motion. He conducted experiments, made calculations, and formulated his groundbreaking laws of motion and universal gravitation. His discoveries revolutionized the field of physics and laid the foundation for our modern understanding of the physical universe.

The story of Newton and the falling apple illustrates how confusion can catalyze innovation and discovery. Instead of just eating the apple and dismissing his confusion, Newton embraced it, allowing it to fuel his curiosity and drive his scientific exploration.

But not all confusion is good; as I mentioned, some dumb people are floating around in this world, and they move a lot, so you keep meeting them often. Here are some signs that your confusion may be a sign of a problem:

- You are unable to make decisions.
- You are having trouble concentrating.
- You are feeling anxious or stressed.
- You are withdrawing from social activities.
- You are having trouble sleeping.
- You are in a negative spiral.
- Your energies are all over the place.
- You are looking for a problem in every solution.

If any of the above applies to you, it's a software problem. As your IT person always suggests, restart the system. But that may not help, you need a software upgrade.

How to upgrade?

A man feeling lost in life goes to see a wise guru. He asks, "Master, how can I find clarity and purpose?" The guru takes him to a window and points outside. "Do you see that tree?" he asks.

"Yes," says the man eagerly.

"And do you see the sky behind it?" the guru continues.

"Yes," the man replies, even more curious.

The guru then takes him to a second window and points out, "Do you see that mountain in the distance?"

"Yes, Master, I see it."

"And do you see the clouds above it?" the guru asks.

"Yes, I do."

The guru smiles and says, "Exactly. You can see clearly."

The man looks puzzled and asks, "But how does that help me find clarity in life?"

The guru pats him on the back and says, "If you can see those things clearly, maybe you just need to clean your glasses. That will give you clarity."

You don't need a six-by-six vision or clean glasses to see clearly; you need a mind that is not cluttered. Clarity is essential because it allows us to make better decisions. When we are clear about what we want, we are more likely to take the necessary steps. We are also less likely to be sidetracked by distractions or temptations. Clarity can also help us to manage our time and resources more effectively. When we know what to do, we can prioritize our tasks and focus on the most important things. This can help us to avoid feeling overwhelmed and stressed. Finally, clarity can help us to build stronger relationships and create a more positive and supportive environment for ourselves and those around us.

How does one achieve clarity?

- Play Dumb: It all starts when we act as if we know nothing about anything. Staying uneducated in a world that constantly tries to educate us is nearly impossible but worth striving for. All we need to do is look at things just

the way they are, not adopt a definition given by society.
- Right Identification: Our mind would circle whatever we identify with. Watching Big Boss and other over-dramatic serials daily won't bring peace to our family life. We want to keep our mind fresh and filled with ideas and positive thoughts. If we don't eat the right food, one will unlikely stay away from the washroom for too long. Conditioning ourselves consciously is like eating the right food.
- Set clear goals: One of the best ways to gain clarity is to set clear goals. We can plan how to get there when we know what one wants to achieve. It all starts with a dream, which culminates into goals, which further culminates into a plan, and then we alter our daily habits to make that plan work. Begin with the end in mind, as Stephen R. Covey wrote in his book, *The 7 Habits of Highly Effective People*. Did you all know that Stephen mentioned that he took inspiration from *Bhagwat Geeta* while writing this book? Well, if you haven't read the *Bhagwat Geeta*, it's time you changed that. No better way to get clarity!
- Get Going: I am successful because I do nothing, claimed no one. Once we have set our goals, we must take massive action meaningfully. We are doing half our job if we continue manifesting and visualizing our goals. Having already achieved something should propel us to take massive action.
- Be patient: It takes time to achieve our goals, and therefore, if clarity is our goal, it will take some time. Therefore, as we create and achieve our goals, don't get discouraged if we don't see results immediately. Just keep acting, and eventually, we will get there.

Common Mistakes

- Never replace clarity with confidence. Confidence is a temporary solution to a permanent problem. Seek until we are no longer confused, and then seek some more.
- Confusion only serves well if we utilize it as a platform to build further clarity; if we allow it to run our mind, causing a lack of decision-making, anxiety, and stress, then it is time to reset.
- Don't seek confusion; that's just being stupid. Seek answers; be a seeker.
- Not every moment is a learning moment. Some moments are to be experienced and enjoyed; never overdo the process. A moment often becomes a memory too soon.
- We may not be completely clear on the subject, but that shouldn't stop us from deciding and acting on it. Remember what Ray Dalio mentioned about human evolution? Once we set higher goals for ourselves, we will likely face problems, diagnose those problems, and design a better solution that gets us going.

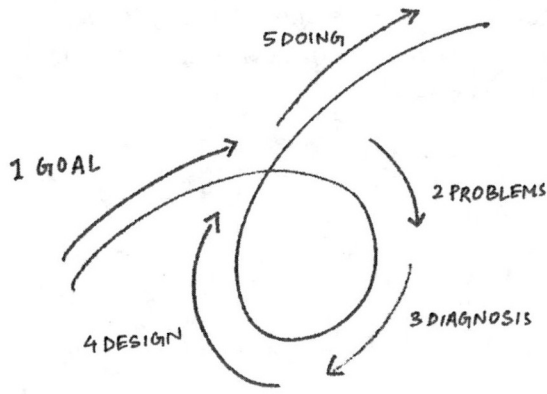

Figure 2: Ray Dalio's Five-Step Process for Achieving Goals

❝ Success Tip

Spend some time away from the world and reflect on what it is you would want to dedicate this life to. What would be the one or two things that you would be proud to be associated with when you look back twenty-five years later in your life? Isolation is not a bad thing, after all. If you are someone who thinks best when they are in their washroom, that's alright; who am I to judge? The key is to be alone and be in a joyful state, which is unlikely to happen in a washroom, so step out and find a peaceful place close to nature.

Take your personal growth to the extreme by venturing into new territories. Join new groups, communities, or classes. Whether it's sports, music, language, AI tools, or personality development, each new experience will ignite a fresh set of neurons in your brain. For instance, my foray into badminton not only improved my physical health but also deepened my understanding of people and my ability to learn new skills. Embrace the adventure of new experiences. But first find your place of solace!

CHAPTER 2

PROBLEMS ARE OBLIGATORY, SUFFERING IS OPTIONAL

IF YOU are an early bird who lived in Mumbai in 2016 and got to board a local train, you might have found someone selling imitation jewelry to passengers on the train. Deepika Mhatre would get up at 4.00 AM every day, get ready, and rush to the local train station in Mumbai not just to sell jewelry but to finish her work in the five homes she cooked in during those days.

But behind all that tedious routine of earning money for her family of five, cooking for five homes, and traveling between Nala Sopara and Malad, Deepika Mhatre has a side that sets her apart from everyone else. She is also a standup comedian.

Sweetly smiling at her audience throughout the act, waiting for the applause to die down after every punchline, Deepika Ji effortlessly wins the hearts of her audience right from the first minute. Each of her jokes feels real, as if a group of domestic helpers is joking about their work and their employers at the end of the day. It is challenging to cushion our daily troubles and channel them through humor, but Deepika Ji does an effortless job. Her tone is always caring, and despite her tedious work routine, she never sounds tired or sad.

If you were to ask her how she changed her career path from domestic help to a stand-up comedian, she would politely reply it wasn't a career change at all; she just found a platform to showcase her talent and help support her family. As her popularity soared, Deepika Ji was inundated with offers from television channels eager to showcase her talent. She was recently honored as one of the "SheThePeople 40 over 40 Awards" 2024 winners. Despite the newfound fame, she remains grounded, driven by the desire to secure a stable source of income for her family.

"My smile is my superpower," she says confidently, showing how something as simple as a smile can help us navigate life's ups and downs. Deepika Ji's story inspires women everywhere who dare to dream and pursue their passions despite all the challenges and looking at that ray of light that pierces through a cloudy day.

Regarding a clouded time, COVID-19 was not the first pandemic to hit our world; it certainly won't be the last. Many pandemics in the past wiped out generations, like the Spanish Influenza of 1919, which resulted in an estimated 25 million deaths. But for this generation, COVID-19 was like a standout event, and we are unlikely to forget about it during our lifetime. However, the question is, would they remember the lessons that came out of this event?

For the majority of us, the answer is NO. That's because we are not conditioned to think like that. We were never told growing up that situations like this would come our way, that we would not be asked if we wanted to participate in it or not, and that it would just happen. Most importantly, we didn't have an option to ask: Why is this happening to me?

Life is a series of situations, one after the other. We do not have an option to choose if they will happen to us; the only option is to view them as either a crisis or an opportunity. If we look for an opportunity in every situation, then we will be able to harness our true potential and grow. On the contrary, if we view them as another enormous crisis, we will limit our exposure to life and withdraw into our little cocoon.

As Ryan Holiday put it so beautifully in his book, *The Obstacle is the Way* and I quote:

> Perceive things as they are, leave no option unexplored, then stand strong and transform whatever can't be changed. They all feed into one another. Our actions give us the confidence to ignore or control our perceptions. We prove and support our will with our actions.

Two friends are hiking in the mountains when they come across a beautiful, serene lake. One friend sighs deeply and says, "Look at this stunning view. It's so peaceful and inspiring. It makes you feel so small in this vast universe."

The other friend nods, pulls out his phone, and says, "Yeah, it's got five bars of signal! I can finally stream the game in HD!"

Now, are you a nature person or a gaming person? You can be both, but you must choose wisely when it comes to choosing. Remember, we always have a choice regarding what we want to notice because it's all about perspective. And remember, whatever we notice will automatically expand in our lives because wherever our focus goes, our energy flows. When someone shows us the middle finger, they may not be asking us to screw ourselves; maybe, just maybe, they are showing us the moon. So, look at that beautiful moon and screw the finger.

The biggest lesson on perspective can be found in our *Bhagwat Geeta*. It begins with the theme of sorrow and ends with a positive note on the possibility of ending suffering through self-realization. Arjuna, like any other human being, is prone to the emotion of sorrow in the face of difficulties. He was overwhelmed with grief as he contemplated upon the prospect of slaying his relations to achieve victory on the battlefield, even though he was being assisted in his actions by God Himself in the incarnation of Lord Krishna. With God Himself by his side as a charioteer, a warrior like Arjuna could not deal with his suffering and face his enemies. Imagine the plight of ordinary men and women when they must make difficult decisions that often conflict with their long-held opinions, morals, and values or involve a radical change in their lifestyles.

We believe that we are the body and the mind, that we are subject to the process of births and deaths, that we have relations, and that we are defined by how we look, what we possess, and what we can or cannot do. When we believe that we are physical and mental beings, we suffer from many fears and anxieties. It is like we are simultaneously dealing with two poisonous snakes in the middle of a hostile forest or sailing in a leaking boat in the face of a severe storm.

This tendency of identification with the physical body is so predominant in Western society (the rest of the world is catching up, too) that we have begun to use yoga for our physical well-being rather than for our spiritual alignment. The yoga teachers are no longer the glum-looking bearded sadhus but attractive men and women in skimpy clothes who are more interested in showing off their bodies rather than the techniques. Today, if you have an unattractive physical body and grey hair, you might find yourself unwanted and unsuitable for a yoga instructor job in an institute!

It is not that we should not think about our physical health. It is how we prioritize things based on our short-term goals, narrow-minded thinking, and degrading ourselves as mere physical beings. We should pay adequate attention to our physical wellness, but at the same time also to that which resides within our bodies; which is permanent, stable and, by identifying ourselves with which we can seek: permanence, peace, inner harmony, and fearlessness that are strikingly missing in our society today.

Krishna talks about the importance of going beyond this limited identification with the body and mind, and recognizing our true nature as eternal souls. This understanding helps us find purpose and navigate challenges with wisdom. He mentioned that while performing duties, we must detach from outcomes. Cultivating detachment frees us from anxieties and attachments that lead to suffering. If you are overwhelmed looking at the eight-hundred-page *Geeta*, start with a simpler version, but please start. Twenty minutes of reading the *Geeta* in the morning before you leave for work would give you the courage and commitment to face anything life throws at you. It's like the Captain America Shield, which is always protecting you.

Common Mistakes
- An opportunity may not present itself in the form of a chance; it would only present itself in the form of a situation. We must have an eye for it.
- The young minds of today want everything cooked up nicely in front of them. Sometimes, we need to cook our food. Zomato and Swiggy can't be everywhere.
- Making problems bigger in the head they are. It all

ultimately boils down to the size of us vs the size of the problem. If we are bigger, then we win. This book is all about how we can make ourselves bigger.

- Identifying too much with our physical side. Spending all our time and energy buying clothes, ornaments, spending excessive time at the gym, becoming obsessive about our physical looks to impress others. All these things have their place if done gracefully and in balance but understand that there is another dimension beyond the physical.
- Not showing gratitude for what we have and complaining constantly about what we don't have is a loss-making deal.

Success Tip

Shoonya Meditation

Shoonya Meditation, also known as the "meditation of emptiness," is a powerful technique that helps practitioners achieve deep relaxation, inner peace, and heightened awareness. Shoonya, which means emptiness or nothingness in Sanskrit, teaches you to let go of your thoughts and emotions to experience pure awareness. It pushes you beyond the physical and mental state, allowing you to access your innermost essence. However, the real essence of this meditation is that it helps create a certain distance between yourself as a piece of life and your physical, mental, and emotional dimensions. We all know that there are two ways of suffering, either physical suffering or emotional/mental suffering. And when you yourself separate from your body/mind/emotions, suffering would essentially perish. Yes, there would be pain, but you shall not suffer. And therefore, your perspective of looking at everything alters immensely.

How to practice?

Find a tranquil and comfortable spot to practice without any disturbances. A serene corner in your home or a peaceful outdoor setting can offer an ideal environment for your practice, allowing you to fully immerse yourself in the experience.

Adopt a relaxed position, preferably with your spine straight. You can cross your legs or keep them uncrossed, whichever feels more natural. Put your hands on your lap or thighs in a comfortable position. Gently shut your eyes and focus on your breath. Take several deep breaths. Take a slow breath through your nose and exhale it out through your mouth. As your breath out gently repeat in your head, "I am neither the body nor the mind." Now imagine yourself a little away from your body and mind, floating in the air and observing yourself from the outside. Repeat this pattern for at least five to ten minutes every time you sit.

The idea is to create a certain distance between yourself and your body, mind, and emotions, because, distance brings clarity, just like we got clear that this planet is round when we looked at it from a distance *(even though there are some flat earthers that still exist who believe in the flat earth theory, it's safe to say they are living in their own world)*. Like any new habit, this may seem strange and uncomfortable; however, once you start seeing the long-term benefits, trust me, you will persist. If you want to learn more, you can visit the Isha Foundation website.

CHAPTER 3

LEARNING THE FUNDAMENTALS OF LEARNING

IT WAS July of 1961, and the 38 Green Bay Packers football team members were gathered for the first day of training camp. The previous season had ended with a heartbreaking defeat when the Packers squandered a lead late in the 4th quarter and lost the NFL Championship to the Philadelphia Eagles. The Green Bay players had been thinking about this brutal loss for the entire off-season, and now, finally, training camp had arrived, and it was time to get to work. The players were eager to advance their game to the next level and start working on the details that would help them win a championship.

Their coach, Vince Lombardi, had a different idea.

"This is a football," he spoke

As a coach, Vince took nothing for granted. He began a tradition of starting from scratch, assuming that the players were blank slates who carried over no knowledge from the year before. He started with the most elemental statement of all. "Gentlemen," he said, holding a pigskin in his right hand, "this is a football." Lombardi was coaching a group of three dozen professional athletes who, just months prior, had won the biggest prize their sport could offer. And yet, he started from the very beginning. Lombardi's systematic coverage of the fundamentals continued throughout training camp. Each player reviewed how to block and tackle. They opened up the playbook and started from page one. At some point, a player joked, "Uh, Coach, could you slow down a little? You're going too fast for us." Lombardi reportedly cracked a smile but continued his obsession with the basics. His team would become the best in the league at the tasks everyone else took for granted.

Six months later, the Green Bay Packers beat the New York Giants 37-0 to win the NFL Championship.

The 1961 season began Vince Lombardi's reign as one of the greatest football coaches ever. He would never lose in the playoffs again. Lombardi won five NFL Championships in seven years, including three in a row. He never coached a team with a losing record. This pattern of focusing on the basics has been a hallmark of many successful coaches. (For example, basketball legends John Wooden and Phil Jackson were known for having a similar obsession with the fundamentals. Wooden even went so far as to teach his players how to put on their socks and tie their shoes.)

It is so easy to overestimate the importance of one critical event or one "big break" while forgetting about the hidden power that small choices, daily habits, and repeated actions can have on our lives. Without the fundamentals, the details are useless. With the fundamentals, tiny gains can add up to something very significant.

Simple Ideas, Deeply Understood

Nearly every area of life can be boiled down to some core tasks, some essential components, that must be mastered if you truly want to be good at something.

Fitness: There are plenty of details on which you can

focus on in the gym. Mobility work is excellent. Analyzing your technique can be crucial. Optimizing your programming is a good idea if you have the time and energy. However, these training details will never replace the fundamental question all athletes must answer: Are you counting your reps and noting your weights?

Love: Displays of affection are lovely. It's nice to buy flowers for your loved ones or to spread joy with presents. Working hard for your family is admirable (and often very necessary). It's lovely to upgrade to a larger house, have a fancier holiday, pay for your children's school, or advance to a higher standard of living. But make no mistake, you can never buy your way around the most essential unit of love: showing up. To be present, this is love. Yes, it counts more than the diamond ring.

Web Design: Building a website is like painting on a canvas that never gets full. There is always space to add a new feature. There is never a moment when something couldn't be optimized or split-tested. However, these details can distract us from the essential thing websites do to communicate with someone. You don't need fancy design, the latest software, or faster web hosting to speak with someone. The most basic unit of any website is the written word. You can do a lot with the right words.

Sports – Badminton: When I started playing, it was about putting the shuttle somehow onto the other side court. Naturally, I struggled. With more playing time, research, and guidance from the coach, I understood that almost every sport boils down to skills, stamina, and strength. When I further delved into the fundamentals of badminton, I understood it was all about playing with an aggressive mind; getting your positions right in doubles play, holding your rackets properly, and communicating with your partner. Just by focusing on these fundamentals, everything in my game changed.

Many more…

Mastery in nearly any endeavor is the result of profoundly understanding simple ideas. For most of us, the answer to becoming better leaders, better parents, better lovers, better friends, and better people is consistently practicing the fundamentals; not brilliantly understanding the details.

Trust me, once we have mastered these fundamentals, our appetite for learning will grow, and how we identify with our learning patterns will shift dramatically.

Fundamental 1: Whom do we listen to?

Oprah Winfrey has served as a mentor for so many women. But who has mentored her? One of the women who inspired, challenged, and guided Oprah was poet and author Maya Angelou. "She was there for me always, guiding me through some of the most important years of my life." Angelou taught Oprah the importance of teaching and of paying it forward. Her invaluable life lessons undoubtedly helped Oprah become the source of inspiration for so many others.

Eighty per cent of CEOs said they received some form of mentorship. Throughout our careers, different mentors will learn about various aspects of us. Some may act as cheerful cheerleaders, celebrating milestones with us, while others may offer direct truth when we need it the most. Therefore, collecting multiple points of view can be vital to keeping an open mind and looking at the big picture, and it's essential when making tough decisions.

So, when I ask to whom we listen to, I am asking essentially who we are influenced by.

We are conditioned consciously and unconsciously

depending on whom we come in touch with in the outside world. It starts with our parents, siblings, teachers, close friends, and relatives and extends to social media and our favorite television shows. Human beings are highly influenced and conditioned by their surroundings and the people they interact with. This would shape our beliefs, attitudes, behaviors, and values. Authority figures, such as parents, teachers, religious leaders, and political leaders, significantly influence our beliefs and behaviors. The opinions and directives of authority figures can impact our decision-making processes and guide our moral compass.

Here are some ways in which conditioning occurs:

- **Socialization:** From an early age, individuals are socialized in their respective cultures and societies. They learn their community's norms, values, and expectations through interactions with family members, peers, teachers, and other significant individuals. Socialization plays a crucial role in shaping one's beliefs, attitudes, and behaviors.
- **Observational Learning:** People learn by observing and imitating the behaviors of those around them. We often model our behavior after the actions of our parents, siblings, friends, and other influential figures. That's our monkey DNA acting upon us.
- **Cultural Influence:** Culture encompasses a wide range of shared beliefs, customs, traditions, and values within a society. Growing up within a particular cultural framework exposes individuals to specific ways of thinking, perceiving, and behaving. Certain cultures, therefore, bind individuals, while certain other cultures set them free.
- **Peer Pressure:** Peers play a significant role in shaping our behavior and choices. The desire to fit in and gain acceptance often leads individuals to conform to the

norms and expectations of their peer group. Peer pressure can influence decisions related to fashion, lifestyle choices, interests, and even more significant life choices. That is precisely what is happening in our colleges and workspaces: fancier clothes, gadgets, hairstyles, and even tattoos. There is no end to this.

- **Media and Advertising:** Mass media, including television, movies, social media, and advertising, has a powerful impact on conditioning individuals. Media influences our perceptions of beauty, societal standards, consumerism, and various social issues. Exposure to specific messages and images can shape our beliefs, desires, and aspirations. Therefore, what we eat, what we wear, and how we think are becoming increasingly out of our control. Only a few strong ones can resist. Are you one of those?

Fundamental 2: The four stages of learning cycle

The four stages of competence, also known as the four stages of learning, is a model based on the premise that before a learning experience begins, learners are unaware of what or how much they know (unconscious incompetence). As they learn, they move through four psychological states until they reach a stage of unconscious competence.

a) **Unconscious Incompetence:** In unconscious incompetence, the learner isn't aware that a skill or knowledge gap exists.

b) **Conscious Incompetence:** In conscious incompetence, the learner knows a skill or knowledge gap and understands the importance of acquiring the new skill. It's in this stage that learning can begin.

c) **Conscious Competence:** In conscious competence, the learner knows how to use the skill or perform the task, but doing so requires practice, conscious thought, and hard work.

d) **Unconscious Competence:** In unconscious competence, the individual has enough experience with the skill that they can perform it so quickly that they do it unconsciously.

A simple example could be learning to drive a car. The first few days are horrible; we are short of hands and feet, constantly abusing the world for driving too fast even though we are driving at twenty, the gear seems too hard to find, the accelerator and brake get all mixed up, we know the routine. And this goes for all male drivers, too, who may be too macho to accept. But after a few days or weeks, once we have become more familiar with the car and the road, our fellow drivers become more friendly, and so does the entire process. We can pretty much drive without our hands or feet (don't try, please). Understanding this fundamental learning is critical because we would always be horrible at anything new we start. Just stay on course, and enjoy the ride.

Fundamental 3: The why vs how conundrum

Let's assume we have been tasked with tearing down a wall without being given any reason as to WHY we should do this. We stand there wondering, HOW am I supposed to break this wall? Should I search for any tools or seek any help?

Let's assume our best friend is stuck behind that wall—not the one who cheated with our girlfriend or boyfriend, but our true best friend whom we love. Given this equation, would we wait for any tools or support to bring down this wall? We would try to tear this down in whichever way possible. That's because we have a very strong WHY; therefore, the HOW does not matter.

Understanding the "why" behind something is more important than understanding the "how" because it provides context and motivation. When we know why we are doing something, it is easier to stay focused and motivated, even when things get tough. Additionally, understanding the "why" can help us make better decisions about how to proceed.

For example, while trying to learn a new language, we may quickly become discouraged if we only focus on the "how" (i.e., how to conjugate verbs, form sentences, etc.). However, if we also understand the "why" (i.e., we want to learn the language to travel to a new country and experience a new culture), we are likelier to stick with it.

Here are some examples that will help you in understanding the concept of "why" and "how":

- When trying to lose weight, knowing why we want to lose weight (e.g., to improve your health, to look better, to feel better) can help us stay motivated when we are tempted to give up.
- When we are trying to learn a new skill. Knowing why we want to learn the skill (e.g., to get a new job, to start a new business, or to improve your hobbies) can help us stay focused and motivated when we are feeling frustrated.
- When trying to decide, understanding the "why" behind each option can help us make the best decision. For example, if we choose to get married to fill your loneliness, we will soon get divorced to regain it.
- When deciding about a career choice, understanding our why can vastly alter our course. A few years down the line, we will not regret the ride.

Fundamental 4: Learning Index

Now, let's get some mathematics involved. A learning index is

comprised of two components.
1. Willingness to Learn.
2. Willingness to Accept Change.

Let's assign ourselves a score from 1 to 10 for each, with ten being very willing and one being least willing. We then multiply our two scores, with the high score being 100 (10 x 10). This is your "Teachability Index."

If we have a high "Willingness to Learn" – 9; but a low "Willingness to Accept Change" - 2, our overall score is meager - 9 x 2 = 18/100. This ultimately means that things are not likely to change regardless of the area(s) in our life that you would like to improve—diet, financial circumstances, skills, etc. On the contrary, if our willingness to learn itself is 2 or 3, our desire to change can be a 10, but again, nothing would change. The idea is to self-reflect on both components, the learning and the application part of the learning; which brings transformation.

Author Brian Herbert said, "The capacity to learn is a gift; The ability to learn is a skill; The willingness to learn is a choice."

Common Mistakes

- Giving credibility to people and institutes without doing proper due diligence.
- While our parents, relatives & friends may have your best interest in mind when they advise us something, always test if it's an opinion disguised as a fact.
- Television and media want more viewership, social media wants more interactions, influencers wish more followers and Business institutes want more money. There are always exceptions to the above, people who genuinely work to

improve this world. Search for those exceptions and make them your home.

- Not paying enough attention to our WHY; write this down everywhere we live, even in our toilet, especially in our toilet.
- Giving up before we reach the stage of unconscious competence. Everyone has a learning curve. I still remember my sister's struggles while learning to drive her car. Her struggles became the struggles of the entire city as she continued driving at 40 in the middle of the road. She didn't give a hoot who was honking her from behind. "It's their problem; they should have left earlier from their homes," she would say. But I am proud she didn't give up and is now an accomplished driver. Thank God for this city!

Success Tip

Breakdown the Fundamentals

Look at everything you are trying to learn by breaking it down to the basics. Study some core principles that are critical to the success of that activity. As I mentioned above, it would likely be half a dozen things or less. Before you approach anything new, do your research in identifying these fundamentals. Once you have identified, then attach all your energy towards focusing only on that for a certain time period. Expand your learning horizon only if you have mastered these fundamentals.

I have given a few examples above related to training, sports etc. But if you pay some attention anything can be broken down to fundamentals.

CHAPTER 4

THE RELATIONSHIP & NETWORK CONUNDRUM

REZBIN ABBA'S house in Areekode village of Kerala's Malappuram district is a treasure trove. If you ever visit, you will find a vast collection of exotic chocolates, teas, and even leaves she has collected from around the world. However, her real treasure is several letters lying around her home, full of kind words, personal stories, and words affirming solid bonds.

Interestingly, the 18-year-old has never stepped outside her village or met the people who had sent the gifts, yet she knows almost everything about their lives.

These gifts and letters are all from Rezbin's pen pals, a concept that might not be too familiar to many millennials today.

For three years, she has been writing letters to strangers-turned-friends from 43 countries. She has penned and received 70 such letters; most people send gifts. She says her hobby, which many people find bizarre, stemmed from a depressive episode and that she found solace in letters.

Rezbin was eight when her parents separated, and she and her brother Abik chose to stay with their mother, Raheena Umminiyil. The separation left Rezbin with a void and had the villagers talking about her — she would often be ridiculed or mocked by her classmates and neighbors.

"I was in class 9 when I heard one of my friends address me as an orphan. Mothers warned their daughters against playing with me as I did not have a father. I would cry myself to sleep, and at one point, I stopped socializing altogether," she says.

"I received my first letter from Sara, a Mexican living in the US, in 2018. She had chanced upon my Instagram profile and started following me. I would post many pictures of arts and crafts on my feed, which she liked. So she asked for my address and sent me a postcard for Christmas. The gesture touched me, and I wrote back. That's how it all began," Rezbin, a first-year student of B.Sc. Psychology, says.

"I was so happy to know that a stranger had made the effort to make me smile. I realized two things, one, that our world is beyond our neighbors and relatives, and two, that I am not alone and there are genuine people out there. How could I have not scaled this project?"

After Sara contacted her, Rezbin tried connecting with people from other countries. After talking to them for a few days, she would tell them about her small hobby of exchanging letters. Many people excitedly said they would like to send some as well.

So, what does she talk about in the letters?

"The topics range from crafts to culture, climate, society, school curriculum, food, etc. We can Google such information but hearing it from the horse's mouth makes a difference. I love telling them about Kerala, its customs, beauty, backwaters, and everything else. With some, I even share my personal life and vice versa. I have learned so much from them, including normalizing single parenting," she adds.

Rezbin's friend Maggie from Bulgaria is a globetrotter. After hearing about India and Kerala from Rezbin, she made plans to visit the country with her parents right before the pandemic. Another friend from Turkey writes to Rezbin about her cancer journey.

Given that the art of letter writing is slowly becoming obsolete, it takes weeks before Rezbin receives her letters. But she says the wait makes it more exciting.

She says she no longer cares about what her relatives or friends say about sharing postal addresses with strangers. Fortunately, her mother is very supportive.

"People have gone to the extent of saying that no one will marry a girl who talks to strangers. If there's anything I have realized, people are always ready to spew venom, but I cannot let it get to me. I don't care if others mock me for being old school in this tech-savvy world, as long as it makes me happy," says Rezbin.

It's not a story we hear daily, but it is certainly one we need to hear today. Today, we live in a world where we are too busy to make meaningful connections, where we are connected with only those who can benefit us somehow. If you were a nerd like me growing up, I can relate to how difficult it would be for you to approach someone. I still remember getting goosebumps approaching a girl, even for some work; forget about dating. But let's see how we can make some sense of networking in today's world.

Let's take a hypothetical example of a software engineer fresh out of college, let's call her Deepti Patel. Being an introvert, she has always struggled with making meaningful relationships in her professional and personal space that could help her in the long run. The first thing is to understand that we live in a world where we need the help and cooperation of other people to succeed. **Success may have a different meaning for everyone, but the easiest way to understand**

success is that we design our lives as per our desires. To create a life as per our desires, we need a network of people carrying the bricks and the cement. These people could be our friends and family members who give us emotional and sometimes financial support too *(if you are good at eating away their heads)*. They could be our managers and mentors who guide us through the rugged terrains. They could be investors who act as angels to give us funds to start our dream company. They could be our employees who work day and night to fill in our pockets with profits *(it wasn't meant to come out in a derogatory manner, but you get it; you are earning a fabulous moolah, thanks to them)*.

Now, networking isn't easy, and it certainly isn't on everyone's to-do list. Depending on our networking personality, it can occasionally be time-consuming, downright awkward, and incredibly draining. Especially when our calendars are already overcrowded with work appointments and family commitments, the last thing we want to do is to make small talk with strangers in a social gathering.

But let's try to give this a positive spin and understand that networking is about establishing, building, and nurturing long-term mutually beneficial relationships with the people we meet. Simply put, it's about making friends, not just Facebook friends but the 3 AM friends who are there for you when you need them. This could happen at Starbucks while waiting to order our morning coffee, attending a cousin's wedding, or attending a work conference. We don't have to join several professional associations and attend every networking event that comes our way to be a successful networker. If we take our eyes off our smartphones when we are out in public, we will see that networking opportunities are everywhere.

Now, coming back to Deepti, our very own software

introvert. Here's how Deepti can become a great networker:

Stepping out of her comfort zone: The first thing Deepti needs to do is get out of her comfort zone and look at networking as an opportunity to make friends with no pressure or stress; recognize that networking requires stepping out of her comfort zone. This is about the battle in your head: Do you need to do this, or can I make it happen without it? Trust me, all the Deepti's out there, you need to do this.

A Lady with a plan: Deepti must decide, based on her interests, what networking opportunities are around her, both within her company and the software industry. A conscious effort to attend industry conferences, meetups, and local tech events, even though networking events, would come a long way in engaging with fellow professionals who have similar interests and backgrounds. Deepti can start small and gradually become more comfortable in social settings. But doing some initial research would help. And you don't need a drink in your hand to become comfortable in these settings, but a cranberry juice disguised as wine wouldn't be a bad idea.

Active participation: I still remember being the first one to raise a hand to ask a question when it came to any business event that had a senior guest coming in for an interaction. Trust me, it wasn't the question eating away my sleep, but the fact that I asked it made me stand out of the group and again pushed me away from my comfort zone. Deepti must too actively participate in industry discussions, both online and offline. It could be professional forums, LinkedIn groups, or tech-related communities where she must share her knowledge, ask questions, and contribute to conversations. By showcasing her expertise and actively engaging with others, she would gain visibility and credibility within the industry. Sometimes, it can get irritating, so make sure you get your timing right and not keep everyone waiting for dinner or, even worse, drinks.

Seeking out mentors: Everyone needs mentors; we all think we know the ways of life , but that is not true. If we follow in the footsteps of someone who has been there and done that, it can save us a lot of time and energy. Deepti must understand the importance of having mentors to guide her professional development. She must reach out to seasoned professionals in her field and express her interest in learning from them. Deepti can gain valuable insights, advice, and support through these mentorship relationships, which would help shape her career trajectory. In addition, these mentors could also open the door for her to network with a broader group of people.

Build a few meaningful relationships: This age-old advice has been hammered and rehammered into our minds but does make good common sense. Rather than focusing solely on collecting contacts, Deepti must prioritize building genuine relationships. She must take the time to connect with individuals personally and show interest in their work and aspirations. She can develop a network of supportive peers, mentors, and potential collaborators by nurturing these relationships over time.

Giving back: Even if you don't believe in this giving back business, trust me, you have a wrong understanding of how the social network operates. You will find a complete chapter later on the power of giving, but understand for now that Deepti must believe in the power of giving back to the community.

She can volunteer at tech events, mentor junior professionals, and participate in initiatives promoting industry diversity and inclusion. These contributions would further solidify her reputation as a valuable and respected tech community member.

I have had my fair share of struggles with this networking thing in school and college. If someone asks me to name a girl in my school who was my friend, I will press the NOTA button. Even in college, I remember it was the girls in my group who initiated the conversation and told me about my horrible choice of clothes, but we wouldn't go there. Much later in my working days, I realized that I was not doing myself any justice by sitting in one corner waiting for someone to come over and initiate the conversation. So, my young friends who are in school or college, reading this, who do not have an audience in the play of networking; the actual game is in the middle. Here are some practical advice to get you started early:

Never judge; just be curious: When we are young in our student life, we often judge people by their clothes, attitudes, and life choices. We often refrain from talking to people we perceive as different. But we have all been there; people usually show off to get noticed, don't get too judgmental about the aesthetics and the outer looks of anyone, and get to know them as a person. Move on without regrets if you still find them superficial and do not match your vibe. So, replace your judgment with curiosity; it's good advice for networking and life.

Choose your battles wisely: Everyone has a friend who is famous for their fighting endeavors. When we are young and hot-blooded, we think everyone is beneath us and we can pick up a fight anywhere and anytime. But trust me, anyone with the reputation of being hot-blooded might win a brownie point out of fear; however, they may never build solid, meaningful relationships. Therefore, keeping your mind calm and focused on productive outputs is essential, as we will automatically attract the right people into our life.

Admire the right heroes: Do we remember being swept off our feet while watching a superhero movie and trying to emulate their life somehow? I still remember seeing a Spiderman for the first time, trying to climb the door of my house and falling right off, thankfully without any damage to my body or my reputation since I was alone then. The point is that we love the concept of heroes and often admire them for what they stand for, for their values, courage, and commitment to a cause. But it's essential to choose heroes who live the life they prescribe and have real blood in their veins. Look around and maybe within.

The social media conundrum

This is an important topic, and I have dedicated an entire chapter to helping our young minds create a personal brand by using social media wisely. Too many of us, including the students, misuse social media only for fun and entertainment. Fake relationships, fake friends, and fake connections end up sucking away all your time and energy, which could well be utilized for doing something productive.

Common Mistakes
- Giving credibility to people and institutes without doing proper due diligence. Never give away our freedom to make decisions, never let anyone decide for us, and let our decisions be our responsibility. Too much dependence on our network can also be fatal. That does not include our

parents and loved ones, of course.
- Also, remember that everyone has a story to tell, and we can learn from their story either what to do or what not to do.
- Having too much on our plate can also be concerning. We need not know everything about everyone; a healthy balance is always necessary.
- If we are in a job that does not involve many social interactions, it does not mean that networking is not for us. Our job and social setup may change, and the things we want from life may change. You always have to be ready for that change.

Success Tip

Stakeholder Mapping

In your student life or profession, keeping track of the key people you must work with closely is always helpful. So, even if you don't want to network with the entire world, start mapping the key people within your social and professional circle. Map them based on their level of connection (more score if you are well connected and share a good bond) and criticality (more score if they are currently important to you) of your relationship. Do add their feedback for you (important since this would determine what action items you need to work on; be honest, don't try to sugarcoat) and what action you should take to improve this relationship. Focus on those stakeholders first whose score is higher in criticality but lower in connection. Here is a brief for your reference:

Name..

Nature of Relationship..

Connection Score (1-5)...

Criticality Score (1-5)...

Their Feedback about you..

Action Items..

CHAPTER 5

PRIORITY NUMBER ONE: HEALTH

EVERYONE WANTS to live long, and most of us hope that a magic pill will appear somewhere that will take care of our health without our intervention so that we can eat whatever we like and sleep for as long as we want. I have news: it's time to wake up and welcome ourselves back from the LALA land. No one is coming to our rescue; we must ride our health vehicle ourselves.

In 2018, when hospitalized for pneumonia, Chennai-based MBBS graduate Dr. Anirudh Deepak was told by doctors that he had five years to live. After which, they said, he was 'a ticking time bomb'. Being overweight, there was no guarantee that any doctor could help him.

In a society that judges one based on physical appearance and largely normalizes fatphobia, Anirudh, also had to deal with the stigma of being overweight. "Even as a school kid, I was ridiculed by peers and by people who were supposed to be protecting me in the first place. That does take a toll on your mental health. But I never cared what other people thought about me. What I think about myself and what my loved ones think about me are the most important things. I was comfortable with who I was then and with who I am right now."

Besides lethargy and tiredness, being overweight often leads to several medical issues. "All your lifestyle disorders are because of a sedentary lifestyle and obesity. Even diabetes and hypertension can be lifestyle disorders. There are other factors, but lifestyle also plays a big role," he explains.

So, following his reality check at the hospital, he knew he would have to change his lifestyle. But the problem was where to start and how to shift that mindset. Anirudh says, "I'm a firm believer that no matter how much other people tell you, unless it comes from yourself, you're not going to change. And once that bell rings inside you, you won't be able to keep it quiet at all. You're going to do something about it. I realized I must take stock of my life for future me." His workout also started with small steps. At 195 kg, walking was a task, let alone getting on a treadmill and working for long hours. For five to six days a week, he started with weight training, gradually stepping it up to include cardio.

Since weight loss involves significant behavioral and lifestyle changes, it's often challenging. Motivation gets you started, but it's about consistency. It's like a woodpecker at work. It keeps pecking at the wood; no matter if the branch falls, it keeps going. It's about being consistent over a long period. It's not a sprint; it's a marathon.

In the roughly two years that followed, he lost over 100 kg, going from 194 kg to 83 kg. Today, he works part-time as a fitness coach, guiding others towards a healthier lifestyle.

I am sure we know someone going through the same issues that Anirudh had to go through; maybe that person resembles us when we look into the mirror. The only question remains whether we would wait for the doctor to force the change upon us or take charge of our health like a self-starting car.

I understand that it is easy to overlook the importance of maintaining good health in a constantly evolving world that demands our attention. Walking through the supermarket, we can see thousands of new brands of eatables whose only job is to make us take the shape of our mother earth. These brands are backed up by massive advertising and marketing budgets and some of the industry's best minds. That's why I stopped my trips to these retail storehouses and ordered whatever I needed from home.

However, there was a time when health was the least of my concerns; even though I had been regular to the gym in college, my health fell off the radar. That's when United Nations proclaimed 21 June as International Day of Yoga in 2014. For once, they did a great job.

My dad had been a big advocate of Yoga practice, but it wasn't cool growing up for me, and it's a shame that no one taught me otherwise. If you are someone who thinks Yoga is not for me, I want you to think about it again. Over the last decade, Yoga & Meditation has become a big part of me; it's connected to my physical well-being and equally important in the other dimensions of my life, including the mental, emotional, and spiritual dimensions.

Yoga is not about twisting your body but rather about becoming one with the universe. It is difficult to explain but much more accessible to experience. The whole idea of my second book came about when I adopted Yoga because I wanted people to experience what I was experiencing. I would encourage everyone to reflect on their lifestyle choices by asking these questions themselves:

- How energetic am I?
- How often do I fall sick, and when I have fallen sick, how long does recovery take?

- How regular are my sleep habits?
- What kind of food works for my body? What food makes me sluggish or bloated?
- What kind of exercise or activity connects with me?
- How can I combine losing weight with a fun sports activity?

The answers to the above questions can create a longing to improve our health because whatever gets measured often improves. So, if we feel our energy levels are down throughout the day, it could come down to a lack of essential vitamins and minerals. If we suffer from irregular sleeping habits, it essentially means that we struggle to sleep and then get up on time, it could come down to our addiction to smartphones or the fact that we are not tiring ourselves enough by doing physical and mental work. Either way, as a generation, if we do not improve our lifestyle habits, the repercussions will be severe.

Now let's look at some of the advantages of maintaining your health:

Physical Well-being: One of the most apparent reasons for maintaining good health is due to its positive impact on physical well-being. When prioritizing our health, we experience increased energy levels, improved immune function, and reduced risk of chronic diseases. Regular exercise, a balanced diet, and adequate sleep are fundamental components of a healthy lifestyle that contribute to optimal physical well-being. Later in this book, we will also read how it affects our focus and productivity. Plus, looking at ourselves in the mirror is just an added advantage. The image of a fitter body in our head fills us with the confidence to achieve anything we desire. So, let's give ourselves reasons to have more mirrors in our house.

Mental and Emotional Well-being: Beyond the physical benefits, good health significantly influences our mental and emotional well-being. Research has consistently shown that exercise and physical activity release endorphins, natural mood enhancers. Regular physical activity has been linked to reduced symptoms of anxiety and depression, improved cognitive function, and increased overall happiness. Furthermore, when we care for our bodies through proper nutrition and rest, we provide a solid foundation for mental clarity, emotional resilience, and managing stress effectively. Enough scientific evidence is available on the mind-body connection. Doctors today use mind-body integration while treating patients and consider holistic solutions while treating symptoms.

Quality of Life: Ultimately, the importance of good health lies in the profound impact it has on our overall quality of life. When in good health, we can actively participate in the activities we enjoy, pursue our passions, and maintain fulfilling relationships. Good health allows us to experience the world entirely, without limitations or constraints. It empowers us to engage in physical adventures, travel to new places, and explore new opportunities enthusiastically and with vigor. People spend their entire lives earning money and later do not have the health to enjoy it. We may be staying in a five-star hospital getting treatment, but it's still a hospital, so why leave our health solely in our doctor's hands?

Longevity and Well-being in Later Life: Another critical aspect of maintaining good health is its influence on longevity and well-being in later life. By adopting healthy habits early on, such as regular exercise, nutritious eating, and stress management, we can increase our chances of living a longer and more vibrant life. There is a beautiful story of a woman named Grace, which is mentioned in the book, *The Top Five Regrets of the Dying*, which she narrates to the author Bronnie Ware. Grace expresses her desire not to live a life in which she is untrue to herself. She wanted to do things for herself but kept prolonging her desire. It was much later in her life, after her husband passed away that she decided to spend her time doing what she wanted. Unfortunately, time doesn't wait for anybody and it was too late by then. Her health was not on her side. She had lost all her strength and was bedridden.

While this story is about living a life true to ourselves, it's all about keeping our health in place for as long as possible so that even if it's much later in life, we have the energy and the required intensity to live freely.

Common Mistakes

- Health is a subjective issue that needs constant self-awareness. People often take a break from this issue, hoping that when they return from unhealthy food, alcohol, smoking, or lack of exercise, the damage may be manageable. The problem is that the damage is often not visible on the surface, so we think it's alright. Yes, you are right; it's often more visible around our belly and waist area; there are no notable marks for guessing that. But most importantly, it's visible in our energy and immunity levels.
- Everyone's body metabolism and cell structure is different; stop following a standard diet prescribed online. Please seek help from an expert. ChatGPT may be an expert dietician, but it cannot check our previous history to design a customized diet. Well, maybe by the time you read this book, it will have become that good, but let's not

take the human experience entirely out of the picture. Get up from your computer screen and hire a personal trainer.
- Television & Media want more viewership, social media wants more interactions, influencers wish more followers and business institutes want more money. Be careful who is selling you what in the name of good health. As I write this, we are in the middle of a movement called 'Read the Label,' which means before you buy anything to eat, make sure you read the label first. Check for sugar content, palm oil, and fatty acids used. Many healthy drinks are unhealthy; don't rely on the influencers or television media; rely on your own eyes.
- We cannot visit a dentist every three months and hope our teeth will be in place; we must brush daily. We cannot go to a gym once every month and exercise for eight hours straight to remain healthy; we have to go at least three times a week for twenty minutes. We cannot eat nutritious food for a week and then go out and eat whatever we like in the name of a "cheat diet". We cannot take a bath once every month for three hours straight and hope to stay in a relationship for too long; it just doesn't work. Consistency is undermined today; no matter how small, persistent, efforts can make a significant difference in the long term.

❝ Success Tip

Create a health plan for yourself, which should be a combination of these four pillars:

I. Physical wellbeing-

Physical wellbeing is a combination of food intake and physical movement. In terms of food, capture your diet to see if you are consuming healthy carbs, fats, and proteins in your food. If you are trying to cut down, you would have to reduce the calorie intake and focus on items that fill your belly more but have fewer calories, like fruits, vegetables, eggs, oats, berries, etc. For physical movement, you can focus on exercise and stretching through gym/yoga/sports/dance etc. Even if you don't like any of that, please make sure you turn Japanese. Not physically but rather psychologically. Japanese people are generally lean and fit because they focus on constant movements throughout the day; they may not be doing extensive workouts, but they are always on the move. Ten thousand steps are not a myth!

II. Mental wellbeing-

I don't claim not to have a Netflix or Amazon subscription, but we must know that binge-watching can become addictive. It takes away your productive time and fills your mind with all kinds of crap. Instead, choose to switch to books or educational podcasts. It would benefit your positive conditioning and produce new creative ideas. Even the newspapers and news media are competing with each other to bring more and more shades of negative news into your bedrooms. Stand guard, my friend.

III. Emotional Wellbeing-

I was hopelessly romantic, often waiting for relationships that would never happen. The term emotional fool seems more appropriate as I look at all those moments of rejection and sadness, thinking I am not good enough. You don't have to go through that process. The quality of the relationships you have in your life and your ability to understand other people's emotions directly depend on your emotional intelligence. Therefore, your plan should include how you would work towards self-awareness, self-management, social awareness, and relationship management.

IV. Spiritual Wellbeing-

We cannot have a plan for spiritual inclinations, they are either there, or they are not. However, creating that awareness inside you that there is a way in which you can take charge of your life should give people enough motivation to pursue this dimension. After all, the core of spiritual wellbeing lies in taking charge of your life energies and karma. I am leaving it to this because an entire chapter is dedicated to this; trust me, it's more interesting than you think.

CHAPTER 6

FINANCIAL LITERACY & MONEY CONSCIOUSNESS

MUMBAI RESIDENT Geeta Patil inherited her passion for cooking from her mother but never thought the skills she acquired would be helpful someday. In 2016, her husband, Govind, lost his job as a clerk in a dental laboratory. This pushed Geeta to use her talents to run the house and support the family. She started her venture, Patil Kaki, which offers traditional Maharashtrian snacks and sweets at home. Though she loved cooking, the business idea was born out of necessity.

She made homemade traditional snacks like *modak, puran poli, chakli, poha, chivda,* and so on with minimal investment. But it soon turned out to be successful. Thus, from earning just Rs 12,000 to almost Rs 1.4 crore annually, Patil Kaki is now a successful venture serving over 3,000 loyal customers.

Her venture also gives hope to several women whose husbands lost their jobs during the pandemic. About 75 per cent of Patil Kaki's workforce is made up of women.

This chapter isn't about business ideas; you can watch Shark Tank for that, where Patil Kaki came and secured funding of ₹40 Lakhs for 4% equity. Patil Kaki's website crashed by the way after that episode of Shark Tank India aired.

Today, Patil Kaki's net worth is ten crores. The snacks company is growing slowly and plans to expand into retail chain stores. The brand hopes to have 20,000+ customers associated with it to deliver the product throughout India.

If you search the internet, you'll find inspirational stories of people with the courage and commitment to create something from nothing and help their families meet their financial goals. But this chapter isn't about financial goals either; it's about having the correct association with money.

Money Consciousness

If you grew up hearing about how the wealthy are looting this world and how money is the root of all evil, you are not in the minority. Most parents and relatives consciously or unconsciously instill in young minds a conditioning that despises money; therefore, people never strive to earn it.

What is the conditioning that I am referring to here?

- Work hard, look for a safe job, and keep your head down.
- Taking too much risk is detrimental; play it safe.
- Money is the root of all evil.
- The world out there is filled with selfish and insensitive people.
- Your dream must match your reality.
- Keep adjusting to the situations that come along in your life and learn to live within your means.
- It's alright to blame others for your failures: society, the economy, the company, the government, bosses, business partners, family members, etc.

So, essentially, our desires and conditioning are engaged in a tug-of-war. While we want to earn money to fulfill our wishes, the above conditioning stops us from fulfilling those desires. As a result, we make halfhearted and sometimes fatal efforts to achieve our dreams, but it's never enough.

So, what does money consciousness mean?

It means appropriately identifying with money and not allowing it to control our emotions. Money is simply a tool or an instrument that expands our capabilities to do more. More money gives us more options to perform certain activities that otherwise may not have been possible. Far too many people have fallen prey to this greed for money; something which was a means became an end for them. I am not against earning money; I would encourage people to earn enough for themselves, so they don't have to worry about their survival process. Then, anything that we earn beyond our survival process should be used to make a difference in other people's lives. Simple to understand, not simple to apply. To summarize, if we are conscious about money, we would keep it in our pockets and not let it enter our heads.

Financial Literacy

Now that you have identified with money correctly, the question is, how do you earn money? For that, you would need to become financially literate.

Imagine this: If I had invested twenty-five hundred every month since I turned adult about twenty years ago at a compounded interest rate of eight per cent per annum, which is very conservative, by the way, I would have had about fourteen lacs in my bank account right now. Except that, I never learned anything about investing until five years ago. Now, in the same scenario if I invest about twenty thousand on average every month, I will almost have one crore twenty lacs in my bank account after twenty years: wow, that's a lot of money! And eight per cent is the most conservative rate possible; you can easily make up close to twelve per cent, which takes the figure up to two crore. It's a good time to keep this book aside and open an investment account if you don't have. Choose any platform you like but act now before the idea is old.

Financial literacy is the biggest asset that young minds need to invest in; it essentially means you are investing in yourself to learn about financial assets. From mutual funds to equity to bonds to real estate to gold, there are many options available where you could invest. All it needs is some common sense and a basic understanding of the underlying principle of how these investment options operate.

In other words, it is the ability to understand and manage your money. It includes knowing how to set financial goals, budget your income, save money, invest, and manage debt.

Robert Kiyosaki, who has made the term financial literacy a common terminology, believes it is essential for everyone, regardless of income or education level. He argues that financial illiteracy is a significant cause of poverty and financial problems. Kiyosaki's approach to financial literacy is based on the idea that there are two types of money:

1. Assets: Things that put money in your pocket, such as rental properties, businesses, and stocks.
2. Liabilities: Things that take money out of your pocket, such as cars, houses, and credit card debt.

Kiyosaki advises focusing on acquiring assets and avoiding liabilities. He argues that assets create cash flow, which can be used to pay for liabilities and build wealth over time. He believes that schools should teach financial literacy and that people should take responsibility for learning about their finances.

We may or may not follow his advice; however, what is critical is to understand the knowledge around these key financial instruments. I have not deliberately expanded on these instruments because we know about them already; if you don't, you know where to find them. For me personally my portfolio is spread into equity, mutual funds, and real estate. The equity market has been kind to me. It has not only helped me become almost financially independent (I have a higher target in mind) but also helped me during distress, like paying off my losses in a startup.

Financial Instruments
- Stocks: Stocks are shares of ownership in a company. When you buy a stock, you essentially buy a small piece of the company. Stocks can be an excellent way to grow your wealth over time, but they can also be volatile, meaning their prices can go up and down quickly. Works for all risk types and short term or long-term investors. Once you zero down on your investment strategy, it's not difficult to earn money from the equity markets. However be mindful of its volatile nature.
- Bonds: Bonds are loans you make to a company or government. When you buy a bond, you lend money to the company or government. Bonds are generally considered to be less risky than stocks, but they also offer lower potential returns. Works great if you are moderate to low-risk investor who is looking for long term benefits.
- Mutual funds: Mutual funds are a collection of stocks or bonds managed by a professional. They can be an excellent way to diversify your portfolio and reduce risk.
- Exchange-traded funds (ETFs): ETFs are similar to mutual funds but traded on exchanges like stocks. This

means that you can buy and sell ETFs throughout the day, which can be helpful if you want to take advantage of short-term market movements. They are predictable and good for low-risk investors wanting a flavor of equity market through mutual funds.
- Real estate: Real estate can be an excellent way to build wealth over time. However, it is essential to remember that real estate is an illiquid asset, meaning it can be difficult to sell quickly if you need cash. Requires extensive research and capital.
- Commodities: Commodities are raw materials such as gold, oil, and wheat. They can be an excellent hedge against inflation but are volatile and risky.
- Future & Options: Options are contracts that give you the right, but not the obligation, to buy or sell an asset at a specific price on or before a certain date. They can be a way to make profits if you believe an asset's price will increase or decrease. However, futures & options are very risky and can lead to losses if you are not careful.

These are just a few of the many available investment instruments. Your best investment instrument will depend on your circumstances and risk tolerance. It is essential to do your research before you invest and to understand the risks involved.

Common Mistakes

- Asking for something before we have earned it. Every day, I notice professionals seeking higher increments and bonuses without showcasing the value they bring. As the saying goes, 'If we do more than what we get paid for, we will soon be paid for more than we do.'

- Spending more than we earn and not keeping account of our spending. I have been guilty myself of doing that for too long. Please don't follow my trail; instead, follow your money trail.
- Getting wealthy through any financial investment requires knowledge of the subject, courage to put in the money, and patience to wait for your money to grow. Most people lack one of the three traits, especially the third one. Overdoing something can sometimes be your undoing.
- Not differentiating between good debt and bad debt. Any debt that helps build your asset base is good, and every debt that takes money from your pocket is terrible.

> ## Success Tip

Create a separate account for each of the activities.

Your savings account is where your income flows in and from where the expenses are made.

- Your investment account is where you manage your investment funds. It's the hub for all your investment activities, allowing you to quickly transfer funds to and from different investment instruments.

- Your wealth account is where you can add your savings and profits (choose a bank with high interest on savings accounts).

- Your emergency account is where you keep at least six months of income.

Start today, use this example: You earn One Lac, which comes into your savings account, and you incur fifty thousand expenses. You can transfer thirty thousand to the investment account and ten thousand each to your wealth as well as the emergency account. Use that thirty thousand for investment into equity, mutual funds, bonds, etc. Any profits earned on the maturity of this instrument should go into the wealth account, and the principal should go back into the investment account to search for the next investment opportunity. These numbers are just an indicator; you can play around and see what works. Most importantly, be disciplined and consistent in your approach.

CHAPTER 7

HAVE YOU READ THE USER GUIDE OF THIS MIND?

THE STANFORD Prison Experiment, conducted by psychologist Philip Zimbardo in 1971, aimed to investigate the psychological effects of perceived power dynamics within a simulated prison environment. Zimbardo and his team set up a simulated prison environment in the basement of the Stanford University Psychology building. They recruited 24 male college students to participate in the study, each receiving payment for their involvement. The participants were randomly assigned to either be guards or prisoners. The participants were fully immersed in their roles. The "prisoners" were arrested by actual police officers, booked, and given prison uniforms. The "guards" were given uniforms, mirrored sunglasses, and batons to establish authority. Zimbardo himself took on the role of the prison superintendent. The experiment was closely monitored through video cameras and one-way mirrors.

Zimbardo and his team observed how participants adapted to their roles and interacted with one another. The situation in the simulated prison rapidly deteriorated within a very short period. The guards began to assert their authority in increasingly abusive and dehumanizing ways, subjecting the prisoners to psychological torment and humiliation. The prisoners, in turn, became submissive and compliant, showing signs of emotional distress and helplessness. The experiment was supposed to last for two weeks, but it was terminated after only six days due to extreme and unethical behaviors exhibited by both guards and prisoners. Zimbardo ended the study early after concerns were raised by a graduate student who witnessed the conditions in the simulated prison.

The Stanford Prison Experiment has been criticized for its ethical implications. Participants were subjected to psychological harm without proper informed consent, and Zimbardo's role as the superintendent blurred the lines between researcher and participant. Some critics argue that demand characteristics and the experimenter's expectations may have influenced the participants' behavior. Despite its controversies, the Stanford Prison Experiment remains one of the most well-known and discussed studies about the human mind.

Have you ever wondered how finicky this mind is, how quickly it responds to external stimuli, and how it starts acting weirdly? I recently read how a Japanese man named Toco has transformed himself into a dog after shelling out more than fourteen thousand euros (twelve lakhs) for a custom-made dog costume. He admits that he always had a vague dream of becoming an animal. That's some physiological circus.

But we have all gone through that feeling where we are thinking that our mind probably has a mind of its own. That feeling of constantly fighting with our mind as if it's raging a war against us; forcing it to do something we don't want to do, but it seemingly responds like a problematic child throwing tantrums at us. I still remember that horrible thought in my head while growing up if I was gay since I could not be with a girl for an extended time period. For a few good months, that thought would not leave me. Don't bother guessing; I am straight, but it were just a weird few months.

In yoga, the human mind is referred to as *Markat*, or monkey mind, because of its nature. The word "monkey" has also become synonymous with imitation. If you say you are monkeying someone, it means you are imitating someone – this is the full-time job of your mind. So, an unestablished mind is referred to as a monkey. In the *Bhagwat Geeta*, Krishna talks about the qualities of a Yogi. He says that the purpose of practicing Yoga is to control the mind. Till such time as we maintain the mind, we shall be dictated by lust, anger, illusion, envy, and greed. That affects our judgment, leads to inappropriate actions, resulting in hatred and restlessness, and makes us weak and irresolute. On the other hand, a calm, peaceful mind is a source of constant strength, helping us make correct decisions and walk the right path.

So, how does one learn to manage their mind?

Identification

Start identifying with the right things; whatever we expose our mind to it will become its raw material to process information and formulate ideas. If we want to become a successful entrepreneur, start exposing ourselves to people in this field, read books on the subject, and research how to build successful companies. Instead, if we constantly expose ourselves to Netflix series around horror or murder mysteries, we are feeding our mind with fear and negativity. Starting and building a company requires a mindset that is not immune from fear but knows how to process the fear factor and proceed anyway.

Before Microsoft became a success in the 1980s, Bill Gates struggled with self-confidence and feared that his business would be a bust; he told students during a Q&A at Harvard, "Even the idea that Microsoft would be a big company, I never would admit that to myself," Gates said. Until his old friend and future business partner Paul Allen convinced him to pursue computer programming seriously, Gates wasn't planning for a career in tech or business. After seeing the first computer with a microprocessor in person in Harvard Square, he decided "It was time to drop out and go build Microsoft to be the first in that business," Gates said.

The decision required a severe mental shift. "So you know, that idea of being an academic to being a CEO, manager, leader type, that sort of developed over time," Gates said.

Notice the above journey carefully; it was only when Bill identified himself with the right ecosystem (computer programming) and with the right people (Paul Allen) that his mindset changed. Let's ask ourselves, what do I identify with? If we are overthinking about sex, maybe it's time we started working on our internet choices.

Stand guard on our mind

Be aware of our thoughts and emotions. The first step to using the mind effectively is to be mindful of what is happening in our head. What are we thinking? How are we feeling? Once we know our thoughts and emotions, we can start channeling them. The problem with controlling something is that we believe it requires a lot of effort; therefore, do not even try it; instead, channel it through the following methods:
- Meditation is a very relaxing exercise for the mind. It helps to improve concentration and focus.
- Alarm Method- It is straight forward: remember that when our mind gets diverted from the present and wanders off into the past or future, try to do some small action,

like snapping your fingers or clapping your hands, to stimulate our mind to get back to the present and focus. Like Rancho said in the movie *Three Idiots*, "All is Well."
- When we get thoughts of what we don't want, try to reverse them, think of what we want, and consider what we wish as an absolute fact. When we think of what we want to do as an absolute fact and believe it is ours, it will simply manifest in our lives.
- Walk, walk, and then walk some more. Let your mind wander while we do that; the best ideas come during times of focus less wandering.

Law of Replacement

Many universal laws operate in this universe, including the law of replacement. We must understand that we cannot eliminate negative thoughts from our mind since our mind only understands sums and multiplications. There are no divisions or subtractions in our mind. That's why if we don't want to think of something, that is the only thing we can think about. We can only replace our existing negative thoughts with positive ones by applying the law of replacement. Here are some basic guidelines:

Learn new things - Learning new things keeps our minds active and engaged and helps us see the world in new ways. When we learn new things, we expand our horizons and open ourselves to new possibilities.

Spend time in nature - Nature has a calming effect on the mind; when we spend time in nature, we are more likely to be relaxed and focused. Go outside and enjoy the fresh air and sunshine.

Start assigning a more empowering meaning to every new experience - Words are powerful and can transform us. However, the meaning we assign to these words is even more powerful. Let's assume someone is cursing us in a language that we cannot comprehend. Therefore, those words have no meaning for us. Thus, instead of assigning a disempowering meaning to our daily tasks, start assigning a meaning that propels us to take immediate action because we are excited about that task. Here are some common examples:

Current Meaning	New Meaning
This is too hard for me.	This is new, and I am learning.
I am the worst at this.	I am not the best person to do this, but I must try for my best; it's a process, not an event.
I'm a bad person.	I have values and principles. A wrong moment does not make me a bad person.
I made a massive mistake, and everyone saw it.	A perfect human being does not exist. No one will even remember tomorrow what happened.
I can't do this.	I can do this, but I might need to a step back, re-evaluate and start again.
I am not good enough.	I am good enough; I am just going through a storm, and the sun will shine soon.
Nobody likes me.	I am loved by my friends, my partner, my parents, my pets...
I'm alone.	I'm not alone; I have God by my side. And that means I have everyone by my side.
I'm a failure.	I wouldn't have known how to grow if I hadn't made that mistake. I know what to do differently next time.
I'm having a breakdown.	I know it's tough, but this might be part of a breakthrough.

Law of Association

The people we surround ourselves with can significantly impact our attitude, behaviors, and beliefs. When we associate with positive, supportive, and motivated individuals, we are more likely to be influenced in constructive ways that encourage personal growth and success. Being around people who share similar goals, ambitions, and values is essential and can be motivating and inspiring. Surrounding ourselves with driven and ambitious individuals can encourage us to strive for our own goals and push beyond our limits.

Buddham saranam gacchami Dhammam saranam gacchami Sangham saranam Gachhami:-

The third verse describes that if you can't be with the Guru or his teachings, at least be with people on a path you want to be. Take refuge in good people. We will associate with good people in life who are virtuous and virtuous people who walk on the right path.

Common Mistakes

- Sometimes everything in this universe is going great, but just one negative thought or issue leaves us wondering if this life is even worth it. The weight of this negative thought is so burdensome that we cannot seem to do anything productive that day. Many of us would have tried to eliminate this negative thought by thinking about another thought, but it doesn't work that way. Just get busy in being busy but towards a more productive work.
- Managing our mind is like managing our time or money. It will only work if we invest some time in understanding the process, do not cut corners, and take the complete course.
- Sometimes, we all need help if we struggle to understand

something; if we think our mind is playing games we don't understand, ask for help. We have an entire chapter dedicated to this later.

- We don't keep hitting people all the time, do we? Our hand is not constantly swaying in the air; we use it when we want. Similarly, if we are not using our mind, keep it aside. Most importantly, don't make it our enemy, and don't try to undermine the importance of this beautiful instrument that we have been blessed with after millions of years of evolution.
- Train it well; don't let it rot in the corner. Think of our mind as a soldier, and you are like that captain in the command center who instructs the soldier on what to do depending on the situation at hand. It would work for us if it has been trained well and then let it do its job without too much interference.

Success Tip

Imagine a life where you're always on the brink of something exciting, where each day is a step closer to a new adventure. This is what it means to keep yourself in a 'crescendo mode'. Intriguing, isn't it?

It means you are always looking forward to the next thing in your life. It could be a destination you are planning to go to, a new dance form or language you want to learn, a new business idea you are planning to explore, or the next child you are planning to have (not relevant if you are a student), but you get the point.

Being in a crescendo mode would keep your mind fresh, and your energies would be channeled in the right direction to make it happen. This way, you would not allow your mind to dictate terms and would always be in mission mode.

CHAPTER 8

FAILURE IS A VIRTUE

WHEN WAS the last time we failed miserably at something and celebrated that as a success? Let me guess, never. We aren't conditioned to think like that because we were all taught growing up that a failure is a failure, but what if that's not true?

I am not asking you to fail intentionally; I am merely asking you to rearrange your definition of what it means to be a failure.

We all love the Amul cartoons, don't we? But had it not been for one man's resilience, those cartoons would never have come to light. Dr. Verghese Kurien, often referred to as the "Milkman of India," was born in Kerala, India. He graduated in Mechanical Engineering and later pursued a scholarship to study at Michigan State University in the United States. Upon returning to India, he joined the newly established Amul Dairy Cooperative in Anand, Gujarat, aiming to modernize and improve dairy farming practices.

When he started working in Amul, Kurien faced numerous challenges. Farmers were exploited by intermediaries who purchased their milk at low prices, leaving them in poverty. Despite his efforts, Kurien's initial attempts to create a cooperative were met with skepticism and resistance from local authorities and farmers.

In the face of adversity, Kurien's determination grew more robust. He partnered with another visionary, Tribhuvandas Patel, to mobilize farmers and establish the Kaira District Cooperative Milk Producers' Union Limited (Amul). Kurien's leadership and relentless efforts turned Amul into a model of cooperative success.

Kurien's crowning achievement came with the "White Revolution," a transformational movement that aimed to increase milk production and empower farmers. He introduced modern techniques of milk processing, packaging, and distribution. The cooperative model he developed ensured fair prices for farmers and made India self-sufficient in milk production.

Under Kurien's leadership, Amul grew exponentially, becoming one of the world's largest dairy cooperatives. His innovative approach brought prosperity to countless rural families and helped alleviate poverty in the region. Kurien's impact extended beyond India; his expertise was sought internationally to develop dairy industries in other countries.

Dr. Verghese Kurien's journey from initial failures to becoming a driving force behind India's dairy revolution is a testament to his resilience, dedication, and unwavering belief in the potential for a positive change that transformed the dairy industry and the lives of millions of rural farmers.

Failure is often seen as a negative thing but can be a virtue. All successful people in the world have experienced failure at some point. The problem begins when we think of failure as the opposite of success. Imagine a seesaw that we would play on as children. As you can see below in that seesaw, we often imagine failure as the opposite of success, which must be avoided at all costs. What if we could reverse the equation and put success and failure on the same side? Failure is not the opposite of success; it is part of success. This simple alteration could change everything for us in terms of the way we are conditioned towards looking at success and failure.

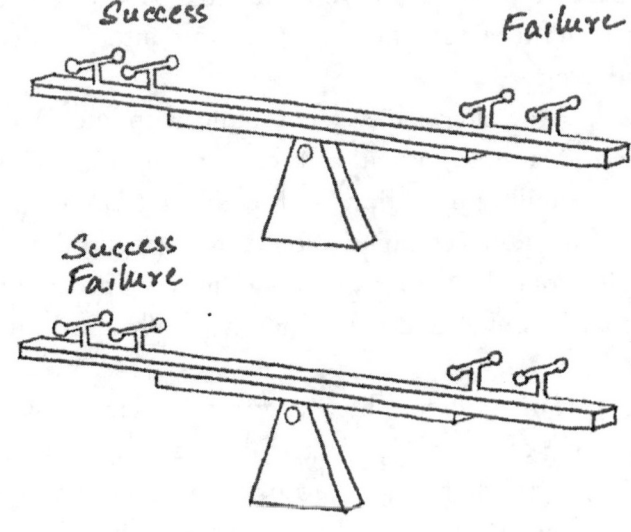

Figure 3: Seesaw of Life

A businessman, known for his frequent failures, finally decides to visit a fortune teller to find out if his luck will ever change. The fortune teller, after peering into her crystal ball, says, "I see that you will face numerous obstacles, experience many failures, and struggle greatly before you finally achieve success."

The businessman, feeling a bit dejected but also hopeful, asks, "So, I will succeed eventually?"

The fortune teller nods, "Yes, you will. But it will be at the very end of your journey."

Encouraged, the businessman asks, "And what happens after that?"

The fortune teller gives him a mysterious smile and says, "Then, you'll write a best-selling book about how you succeeded, and everyone will forget about all your failures."

The businessman, puzzled, asks, "Why will they forget my failures?"

The fortune teller laughs softly, "Because, in the end, success has a way of making failures look like mere stepping stones."

Failure as a stepping stone or an indicator of success!

If we are not failing enough it could mean we are in our comfort zone and not allowing ourselves to grow. All growth can happen outside of our comfort zone. I have had the fantastic experience of working on two startups, and seeing them fail wasn't easy, but there is so much that I have learned from that experience. If we want to learn from experiences, go to a place where you get instant feedback so we can fail fast. That is the best part about sports, we get instant feedback if we have succeeded or failed. Sometimes, in college or professional life, we must wait until the year's end to get feedback on our performance, defeating the entire objective.

While we may be failing because we suck at something, or we are not giving it our best shot because we have no interest. If that is the case, we must first find something interesting. But if we are doing something we enjoy, like sports, music, entrepreneurship, writing, or public speaking, we could look at a concept known as conscious practice. While regular practice might include mindless repetitions, conscious practice requires focused attention and is conducted to improve performance. Therefore, one needs to monitor the progress and get constant feedback from an expert; it means one must practice till they have failed, get feedback, and then go again.

How to bounce back?

- Allow yourself to feel your emotions - Feeling disappointed, frustrated, or even angry after a failure is okay. Don't try to bottle up your emotions. Allow yourself to feel them, and then let them go. Talk to someone if that helps, but don't live in the past.
- Reflect on what went wrong - What factors contributed to your failure? What could you have done differently? This will help you learn from your mistakes and avoid making them in the future. This is where conscious practice comes into the picture; you need someone to guide you on what you are doing wrong, maybe someone who has been there and done that.
- Set realistic goals for yourself - If you set unrealistic goals, you're more likely to fail. Set goals that are challenging but achievable. This will help you to stay motivated and avoid disappointment. Sometimes, in haste, we go from gear one to gear four, which would break down your vehicle. Gradually progress, and let no one dictate your pace.
- Take breaks - When you're feeling overwhelmed, it's essential to take a break. Please leave the situation and return to it later with fresh eyes. Do something that takes your mind away from the task. A walk, a date with your partner, a holiday, or even some sleep can help.
- Celebrate your successes - This is perhaps the most important thing. Sometimes, when climbing 10,000 stairs and feeling tired, look back; maybe you have already climbed 3000, so take a break and have a KitKat. You see, even small successes are worth celebrating.

When success becomes fatal

There is another side to this equation, where one forgets about failures because everything is going great. It could make us take things for granted and become overconfident in our abilities. The best of organizations have suffered the worst of fates when they thought they were too big to fail. History offers several cautionary tales of organizations that, despite their size and influence, ultimately succumbed to financial collapse because they took things for granted. This should serve as a stark reminder of the potential consequences of overconfidence and complacency.

Eastman Kodak, a pioneer in photographic film, was synonymous with photography for most of the 20th century. Despite inventing the first digital camera in 1975, Kodak failed to embrace digital technology, fearing it would cannibalize its film business. This resistance to change led to a steady decline in market share. Kodak filed for Chapter 11 bankruptcy protection in 2012, underscoring the peril of failing to adapt to technological advancements. Similarly, Blockbuster, the video rental giant, was dominant in the home entertainment industry during the 1990s. At its peak, Blockbuster had over 9,000 stores worldwide. However, the company failed to adapt to the digital revolution and the rise of streaming services. Once an upstart DVD rental service, Netflix offered to sell itself to Blockbuster for $50 million in 2000. Blockbuster declined the offer, and by 2010, it filed for bankruptcy, unable to compete with Netflix's innovative model. These examples highlight the importance of adaptability and the need for continuous learning in the face of changing times.

A young man goes to an old, wise guru searching for the secret to success. The guru tells him, "Meet me at the river tomorrow at dawn, and I'll show you."

Curious and eager, the young man arrives at the river the following day. The guru takes him into the water until they're waist-deep. Suddenly, the guru grabs the young man and pushes his head underwater.

Panicking, the young man struggles to breathe, but the guru holds him down. Just as the young man feels he can't take it anymore; the guru pulls him up. Gasping for air, the young man shouts, "What was that for?"

The guru calmly replies, "When you want success as badly as you wanted to breathe just now, you'll find it."

Drenched and shaken, the young man says, "That's a powerful lesson, but what about failure?"

The guru smiles and says, "Failure is what happens when you get so focused on success that you forget to come up for air."

Ask yourself if you want success as much as you want to breathe, and also ask yourself if you are coming up again to breathe without getting lost in your success.

Common Mistakes
- We may be over-emphasizing our failures and undermining our successes. Too many people do not give themselves enough credit for their successes and are often too hard on themselves if something goes wrong. Ideally, we must disassociate ourselves from success or failure and focus on getting the process right.
- Over-indulgence in the outcome as compared to the process. We should be obsessed with the process and not the outcome.
- Overworking and not giving ourselves enough time to

reflect if something hasn't worked out. Sometimes, the best way is to take a step back, take a break, reflect, and go back with a better plan.
- Not associating with the right people and not seeking enough help. If you think you can do everything independently, think again.

Success Tip

Create for yourself a failure reflection form, something that showcases your list of failures. This was a technique that Ankur Warikoo made famous when he put out his "failure resume" for everyone to see. You need not go so far as sharing the list with everyone, but creating a list for yourself would help you become more mindful of what hasn't worked for you in the past. That may be due to a combination of various factors, some of which may not be in your control; however, if you can, pay some attention to those variables that could have altered the situation in your favor. Reflect on what you could have done differently under the circumstances.

Don't just stop there; also list your achievements on the next page so that you know you have it in you to make it to the top. All the failures in the world cannot stop you in your journey.

CHAPTER 9

SPIRITUALITY IS FOR EVERYONE

A VERY remarkable incident occurred in Vivekananda's life. One day, his mother was very ill and on her deathbed. Now, it suddenly struck Vivekananda that there was no money in his hands, and he could not provide her with the necessary medicine or food. It made him very angry that he was unable to take care of his mother when she was sick. When a man like Vivekananda gets angry, he gets furious. He went to Ramakrishna, his Guru since there was nowhere else to go; even if he got angry, that was where he would go.

He told Ramakrishna, "All this nonsense, this spirituality, where is it getting me? I could have cared for my mother if I had been employed and done what I was supposed to do today. I could have given her food, medicine, and comfort. Where has this spirituality taken me?"

Ramakrishna, a worshiper of Kali, had a Kali shrine in his house. He said, "Does your mother need medicine and food? Why don't you go and ask the mother for what you want?" It sounded like an excellent idea to Vivekananda, so he entered the shrine.

After about an hour, he came out, and Ramakrishna asked,

"Did you ask the Mother for food, money, and whatever else your mother needs?"

Vivekananda replied, "No, I forgot."

Ramakrishna said, "Go back inside again and ask."

Vivekananda went into the shrine again and came back after four hours. Ramakrishna questioned him, "Did you ask the Mother?"

Vivekananda said, "No, I forgot."

Ramakrishna again said. "Go inside again, and don't forget to ask this time."

Vivekananda went inside and, after almost eight hours, came out. Ramakrishna again asked him, "Did you ask the Mother?"

Vivekananda said, "No, I will not ask. I do not need to ask."

Ramakrishna replied, "That's good. If you had asked for anything in the shrine today, this would have been the last day between you and me. I would never have seen your face again because an asking fool does not know about life. An asking fool has not understood the very fundamentals of life."

Are you one of those who think spirituality is only for the dying? I don't blame you because, unfortunately, the word has been corrupted over many years of use and misuse, but let me say it for you:

a) Being spiritual means becoming a seeker who does not believe anything but knows everything through experience. That's why whenever I address my audience anywhere, I often include a disclaimer for everyone: Do not believe anything I say, but at the same time, do not disbelieve it either. Become a seeker instead, use these ideas, and explore them further.

b) Being spiritual means taking charge of life and believing my life is my own or karma. This empowering thought ensures we do not let challenging situations bother us too much.

c) Being spiritual means not reacting to any situation that life throws at us; instead, we patiently observe and respond consciously.
d) Being spiritual means exploring the deeper meaning of life and death, so we don't take this life for granted.
e) Being spiritual means questioning everything about God and to God himself, just like Arjuna asked Krishna. Remember, in this culture, there are no commandments.

Now, look at our present life and situations. Do we need spirituality, or do we not? Do not let our so-called cool friends talk us out of it. Spirituality is for everyone!

The other side of the story is that far too many people who have tried to walk the spiritual path are drawn away from it due to social pressure. When we mention to our loved ones that we are on a spiritual path trying to make meaning for this life, they worry for us instead of being happy. This is because society has labeled spirituality as a taboo that is reserved only for those who wish to stay in the jungles or ashrams. According to society today, these people wear orange or red rubs, and most have shaved off or grown a long beard. They think the path of spirituality is reserved for only a few people who are willing to sacrifice all their social lives to pursue some stigma.

Being spiritual is a longing for every human life; it's just that most people do not pay enough attention. Instead, they try to balance this longing for something by purchasing fancier assets like jewelry, cars, or houses.

Do not get me wrong. I have no grudges against anyone collecting these assets. However, it's essential to know their place in life. The trouble starts when we become dependent on these assets, and instead of owning them, they start owning you.

You see, the more we identify with all our different roles, the more we move away from our source of creation. Instead, if we take on one single identity, which is a piece of life itself, we can easily create a distance between ourselves and the roles that society expects us to play. Please don't take me as wrong; I am not implying that these roles are unnecessary or that we must move away from these social responsibilities, therefore don't use this book as an excuse to break up with your partner.

The Yogi walked into the Pizza Parlor and said: "Make me one with everything." When the Yogi got the pizza, he gave the owner of the place 200 rupees. The owner happily pocketed the amount. The Yogi said, "Don't I get any change?" The owner said, "Change must come from within."

Remember, laughter is like a little dose of enlightenment for the soul. Being spiritual also means taking in all these daily doses.

Meditation

My daughter came to me once after she saw me meditating one morning and asked if she could join me. I said, of course, and advised her to close her eyes and try to focus her attention on her favorite God; remember, she is just six years old. I was pleasantly surprised when I peeked to look at her after five minutes. Her eyes were still closed, and her face had a certain sense of grace, joy, and calmness. I asked her about her experience, and she politely mentioned that she enjoyed herself but would prefer to play, and in a whiff of a moment, she was gone. All I heard afterward was her wholehearted laughter as she played with her toys. For me, she is the epitome of grace, joy, and calmness. God has blessed me with her presence because, at that tender age, she is mature and childish at the same time; she is calm and energetic at the same time; she is straight and naughty at the same time; she is clear and confused at the same time, but most importantly she is already meditative without doing any meditation.

We think meditation is a task we must accomplish every day by forcing ourselves to sit in a certain way and stay focused without thinking about anything. This idea of being disciplined in our manners and routines makes many people run away from meditation. In reality, you don't do meditation but rather become meditative. The whole day is a way to prepare ourselves to sit quietly for those twenty minutes in gratitude and self-reflection.

The Bhagwat Geeta

Whatever your background, affiliation, religion, beliefs, or aspirations are, please spare some time to read the *Bhagwat Geeta*. It talks about the four paths that every human being must walk:

I. The Path of Devotion or Bhakti Yoga—Devoting everything one does to the almighty. Remember, devotion can go wherever willpower cannot take us; it is one of the most underestimated forms of intelligence.
II. The Path of Wisdom or Jnana Yoga – Learning something new daily to become our best version.
III. The Path of Discipline, or Sadhna, is a daily reminder to stay on course and not lose our way.
IV. The Path of Service to Others or Sattvik Karma—Taking everyone along. Once we have enough, it's essential to think of others. A fancy car won't create the satisfaction that our soul needs.

Spirituality is Empowerment!

It empowers us by giving us the clarity to proceed in life and helping us build up the necessary faculties to remain unfazed no matter what situation life throws at us. Most people fear taking the next step because they fear it will bring them discomfort. However, if you have fixed this life in a way that no matter what life throws at you, you are ready, then you can carry out more and more activities without worrying about the consequences. Our level of activity in this world is not curtailed in any way by our fear of being in discomfort either physically or mentally.

Next time you board a train, remember that we don't continue to carry our bags on our journey. We keep it aside and pick it up when we reach our destination. We only access these bags if we need something from them and then put it back again. Now replace the train journey with our life's journey, replace those bags with our body, mind, and emotions, and finally, replace the passenger with ourselves as a piece of life. Our only identification with our body, mind, and emotions should be when we need access to them to perform certain activities. For example, I am trying to access the limited intelligence of my mind and the depth of my emotions right now to complete this book. Let's do ourselves a favor and keep the luggage down on this journey called life.

Common Mistakes

- Over complicating the process, remember simplification is a great friend.
- We have many spiritual readers in this world, and we need more practitioners. Spirituality is for one to experience; no matter how much I write about it, we must try to explore this dimension by practicing.

- A religious person believes in whatever the religious preachers say; a spiritual person does not feel anything; he seeks to understand the truth. For him, no higher authority is telling the truth; the truth is the only authority. A spiritual seeker can always be religious; we don't need to choose one.
- There is no need to leave our present ecosystem and leave for the ashram or the Himalayas to become spiritual. It all starts with building an ecosystem that supports our growth as a human being, in all ways trying to become the best version of ourselves.
- We can always do this alone, but being with a spiritual master would help speed up the process, just like we can learn to play cricket ourself, but a coach would help us become better much more quickly.

Success Tip

The One Name Sheet technique

Please pick up a sheet of paper and write down the name of every person or entity like the government, your college, your company, your boss, your teacher, your friends, your country (remember it's not mandatory to start with your spouse or your partner) that you think is responsible for you not being able to live the life that you want live. They would include those names you would like to blame for your failures. Now, do yourself a favor; for once, read these names aloud and bless them for not being there for you when you needed them. Bless them for teaching you the most invaluable lesson: "Your life is your own making."

Now, pick up that sheet of paper again and on its back, write just one name - Your Own. Place this sheet where the only name visible to you when you look at this list is YOU. Make it a daily habit to revisit this sheet with your name on it. It's a vital reminder. From now on, every decision you make, take full responsibility for its consequences. Some of you might worry this will bind you, but in reality, it will liberate you. Yes, we still need the support and blessings of this world, and no one can succeed alone. However, shifting the burden of responsibility onto yourself will propel you to take necessary action in the right direction.

CHAPTER 10

DON'T BE SHY TO SEEK HELP: SPEAK UP

MILLER, A former five-star recruit, was a starter in his sophomore year during the Buckeyes' run to the 2020 CFP National Championship Game. He started in Ohio State's Big Ten title win but did not play in the CFP semifinal after testing positive for COVID-19. Miller came off the bench in the national championship game. But this story isn't about his sporting achievements.

To everyone's surprise, Harry Miller revealed that he had attempted suicide. Miller announced his medical retirement from football on March 10, 2023, in a Twitter post shared over 10,000 times.

"I had no intention of this happening like it did," Miller said. "People have called me brave, but it felt like not dying. It felt like being honest. Maybe bravery is just being honest when it would be easier not to, and if that's bravery, then so be it."

Miller survived because he was brave enough to speak to his coach and seek help; however, most young adults today shy away from speaking up.

As per the UCLA Health survey, suicide is the second-leading cause of death among people aged 15 to 24 in the U.S. Nearly 20% of high school students report serious thoughts of suicide, and 9% have attempted to take their lives, according to the National Alliance on Mental Illness. The study mentioned that socially, teens and young adults don't have the same connections as older adults. Someone who is married and has a long-term partner, or has children or grandchildren is socially different than someone who is just coming into their own, living with roommates, or alone. The numbers aren't that great in India, either. In India, the National Crime Records Bureau (NCRB) statistics showed a concerning rise in suicide rates from 9.9 per lakh population in 2017 to 12.4 per lakh population in 2022.

I cannot forget this instant that happened to me. During one of the public speaking sessions at a college, a female student came to me with a query that she had. It was clear from her tone and mannerisms that she had been struggling with this topic for a long time. She asked me, "I am from a small town in UP, and my parents were not keen to have me educated anything further, and therefore, I ran away from them to study here, and ever since then, we haven't been in contact. I always miss them and am unsure how to tackle the situation."

I took a moment to absorb the gravity of the situation; I could see her pain flowing through her eyes, which had become wet as we conversed. I gathered my thoughts as I wanted to make sure that I showed compassion towards her without undermining her parents. So I said: "You must connect with your why every day in some manner."

"What does that mean?" she inquired.

I responded: "There is a reason you ran away from your home; it was because you wanted to build your career and have a bigger impact on this world, I imagine. That is your why. To subdue the pain you suffer daily, you must stay connected to this why. Make sure you remind yourself daily that you are here for a reason; remember that this pain you are going through is temporary, but your achievements will be permanent. Write down your why on a sheet of paper and paste it somewhere you can see it daily. This would give you hope, courage, and commitment to pursue your dreams with passion and vigor. You would see that your pain would falter away not in one day but surely one day."

As she walked away, I could see some hope written on her face. I never got to follow up with her, but I was glad she could open up and seek help by sharing something personal.

It is essential to understand that it's all right to seek help and that there are no medals you would win for fighting your battles alone. You need to seek help, especially in the following areas of your life:

- **Learning and growth:** We can't learn everything on our own. We need the help of others to teach us new things and grow as individuals.
- **Achieving our goals:** Often, our goals are too big for us to achieve on our own. We need the help of others to provide us with support, motivation, and resources. Also, having someone monitor our progress and give us timely feedback can save us valuable time.
- **Overcoming challenges:** Life is designed to create situations that challenge us daily. While we can tackle some of these challenges on our own, we need help with others. We need a mentor, a guide, a friend who shows us the right path, and someone with whom we can speak with without the fearing being judged. For every Miller struggling, perhaps we need a coach who can save our life.

- **Feeling connected:** Humans are social creatures, and we need a connection with others to feel happy and fulfilled. We need the help of others to build relationships, to feel loved and supported, and to find a sense of belonging.

The best part about seeking help is that once we start asking, it would arrive in abundance, and that too from every side:

I. Our family members can provide us with love, support, and guidance.
II. Our friends can provide us with friendship, companionship, social support, and sometimes advice on what not to do in life.
III. Our teachers, mentors, and coaches can provide us with education, training, guidance, and the strategy and plan to achieve our goals.
IV. Our colleagues can help us with industry knowledge, collaboration, and growth opportunities within the role.
V. Our community can help us with opportunities to improve our skills, a chance to be heard, and a sense of belonging.
VI. Our children can guide us on how to stay curious, joyful, and creative.
VII. Our celebrated starts can guide us on how to manage our success with grace and humility.

Becoming a world-class help seeker

The title may amuse us; however, do not underestimate its immense value. Once we start the process, we can improve and influence people to help us. It could be the CEO of our company, that social media influencer we have been following, or the relationship expert who could help us get our perfect life partner; we can always learn how to approach them and

seek help. Here are some guiding points:
- **Be clear and concise:** Often, the people we would approach to seek help would be preoccupied with something more significant to them than helping us. Therefore, once you approach them with a request, please be as precise and brief as possible. Unless they ask for more details, do not start narrating your entire story from when you were born. What do you need help with? The more precise we are about what you want, the more likely people can help us.
- **Give before we receive:** This advice is so valuable that I have made an entire lesson out of it, which you will read later. For now, understand that we need to offer something if we seek help from someone not within our private or social circle. If we are writing to your favorite YouTuber seeking a collaboration opportunity, now think about what we can provide to that person who probably receives a hundred such requests daily; why should he pay attention to our request? We may mention something like this in our email request:

Dear Mr. X,
I have been your most ardent follower and even purchased your course, which I found immensely valuable for my personal growth. I am seeking your collaboration on a podcast, which I think would be of great value to our followers. While my total follower count is low now, I would spread the word on your videos and books if we could collaborate.

- **Explain why?:** Explain how our life would be better if they helped us. People often need to see the picture of the good times to be proud that they contributed to a better world, whether for us or someone else. So, if we are

seeking monetary help from someone for an educational NGO, send them pictures of the happy children studying in the classroom we built or the new sports equipment that we bought for our students.
- **Be respectful and polite:** People are more likely to help us if you are respectful and courteous. Avoid making demands or being pushy. Often, people are aggressive even while seeking help; they think it's their birthright to receive help.
- **Close the loop:** If someone has helped us, always thank them and explain the transformation we have seen in ourselves due to their intervention. This will show that we appreciate their help and that it was not in vain. While we are closing the loop, always offer to be there for them for anything they may need from us in the future; this puts us on equal ground with them and may lead to a possible friendship opportunity if that person is a social acquaintance.

Last but not least, if you enjoy reading this book and would like to seek help with anything I have discussed, I will happily assist you. All my contact details are at the end of the Author Profile page.

Common Mistakes
- Allowing our ego to come in the way of seeking help, please keep our ego aside and be humble enough to accept that we cannot do this alone.
- Seeking help from those who do not have the expertise to help. Asking our friend for relationship advice is not the best strategy if that friend changes his girlfriends every season. Asking our teacher about earning money is not the

best advice if that teacher comes in an auto rikshaw daily. Asking our wife or girlfriend about losing weight is not the best advice…*you get the point!*

- Asking before giving - As I explained earlier, people outside our influence need a reason to help us; they do not love us and may not have even heard of us. Create that reason before we seek any help.
- Be mindful that this does not give us the right to depend on others for things we can do independently. Seek help only if we have exhausted all possible options for doing this task independently.

Success Tip

A resource tracker

A lot of people need help with getting access to the right resources at the time that they need them the most. That is because we haven't planned for such a rainy day. Now, reimagine a world where you have instant access to those resources at the click of a button. All you had to do was search for the topic of your interest, your query, and your prompt.

Yes, I am talking about our very own ChatGPT, which is personalized for our requirements. Start by preparing a list of resources that will help you at the time of your need and keep updating them as your requirements expand. This list could include numbers and email IDs of your network group and their strengths/areas of interest. This could consist of the emergency numbers of your doctors and authorities. This could also include links to essential websites you would like to access to learn something.

CHAPTER 11

HIDDEN KEY TO SUCCESS: INVOLVEMENT

IF YOU follow social media, you would have heard of Revant Himatsingka, the "Foodpharmer."

Growing up in the 90s in Kolkata, Revant had a regular childhood, which included biscuits, packaged foods, and drinks like Bournvita. Like millions of Indians, the young boy was blissfully unaware of the harmful effects of the food he consumed.

He slowly learned the importance of nutrition over the second decade of his life, which he spent mainly in the US. Revant moved to New York for his undergraduate degree in finance and management in 2011. It was also when he started taking an interest in food and nutrition, which eventually cemented with a health coach certification in 2015. He also started reading food labels carefully during his grocery store runs. He soon realized that most companies say something on the front of the pack while the back states a different story. He was angered when he realized that while the company states that the product is natural, organic, and perfect for you, the truth is far from it. This led to intense research on nutrition and food labels over the past decade of his life.

Revant previously worked as a management consultant

at McKinsey & Company. His stint at the management consulting firm, in many ways, laid the groundwork for his content today. Working in consulting meant solving problems in a structured manner. Revant decided to use this skill to help solve the more significant issue of reading and understanding food labels. With this plan in place, he quit his job and returned to India, much to the chagrin of his family.

Because of his efforts, Cadbury reduced the quantity of added sugar in Bournvita by 14.4 per cent in December 2023, validating the content creator's efforts. The Central Government also directed e-commerce firms to remove Bournvita and other such drinks from the health drinks category.

His latest project, "Label Padhega India," is focused on educating consumers about how to read and understand food labels. The initiative aims to inform people about the hidden risks associated with nutritional information on packaged foods, highlighting the adverse effects of preservatives and unhealthy additives on health.

Leaving a lucrative Rs 2 crore job on Wall Street and setting foot on a mission to spark a "health revolution" in the country could not have happened without someone being involved with that mission. The truth is nothing gets accomplished unless we get involved with something. In that zone, we lose focus on all the petty things in life. We no longer care for that lucrative job, we don't care what the world thinks of us, and we don't care about our well-being because what we are trying to accomplish becomes more critical. We know that these short-term compromises would lead to long-term gains.

Bill Gates and Warren Buffet were asked the same question regarding what they would dedicate their success to, and they attributed it to the word focus. Focus comes from involvement; however, it is not something we do but become.

Practicing Involvement

If this was about that girl in our college or our office colleague we adore, would there be a need to teach us how to stay involved with her? When it comes to people, involvement starts with taking an interest in them, caring about them, and doing what is best for them. However, when it comes to our daily routine tasks, involvement could often start with doing something we love, something that could change this world for good, or something that would positively impact the maximum number of people.

We cannot stay involved in economics class because we do not know why this is needed. The professor hasn't cared to explain, the college dean hasn't cared to explain, and our parents certainly haven't cared to explain. But if I were to tell you that many of the concepts in economics could be of immense help for you in your wealth generation. Studying economics can provide you with valuable knowledge and understanding of how financial markets function, which can be beneficial for making informed investment decisions. According to a 2019 investigation in the Harvard Business Review, economists have started playing a much more significant role in the tech sector since 2019. Tech companies, including the big boys like Amazon and Google and smaller startups, have begun to hire groups of economics PhDs. Then, would you be suddenly interested in pursuing economics, even if it's tedious or unrewarding to start? Still, you know that many long-term benefits overshadow the short-term challenges.

On one extreme, there is involvement; on the other, there is attachment. People get so attached to someone or something that they do not see an alternative when it's taken away from them.

Known as a value manager who favored undervalued and unloved stocks, de Vaulx was named Morningstar's

International Stock Manager of the Year in 2001, along with his long-time mentor, Jean-Marie Eveillard. He was a runner-up for the same prize in 2006. In 2008, de Vaulx joined International Value Advisers and served as chief investment officer, co-portfolio manager, and partner, building it up to be worth more than $20 billion in assets at its peak.

In March 2021, International Value Advisers announced it would liquidate its funds and close up shop because its assets under management had collapsed from $20 billion to under $1 billion as a result of client redemptions, attributed in part to a generalized slump for the value investing strategies de Vaulx favored. Another report, however, claims that the firm still had more than $2B in assets, and "value was beginning to see a resurgence." On 26 April 2021, de Vaulx committed suicide by jumping from the 10th floor of the International Value Advisors office building.

This is a classic case of someone attaching their life to the company they owe. Mr. de Vaulx forgot that he owned the company, not vice versa. That is the trouble when people get so attached to their assets that they forget there is a difference between life and lifestyle.

So how does one stay involved yet not get attached?

The word you are looking for is—Detachment

According to *Bhagwat Geeta*, detachment is more than a lack of attachment to material things. It is a state of mind in which we are not attached to anything, including our thoughts, emotions, and desires. In the *Bhagwat Geeta*, detachment is seen as a necessary condition for achieving moksha or liberation from the cycle of birth and death. Krishna explains to Arjuna that he must fight without attachment to the outcome. He tells Arjuna that he should do his duty without

worrying about the results because the results are not under his control.
- Detachment is not about being indifferent or apathetic. It is about being free from the ego, the source of all our attachments. When we are attached to something, we identify with it and see it as part of ourselves. This can lead to suffering because we become attached to the things we have, the people we love, and the ideas we believe in.
- Detachment allows us to see things as they are without the filter of our ego. This will enable us to act more balanced and compassionately and experience greater peace and freedom.
- When detached, we are less affected by life's ups and downs. We can maintain a sense of peace and equanimity, even in the face of challenges.
- Detachment allows us to be free from the ego, the source of all our attachments. This will enable us to live more authentically and follow our true calling.
- Detachment allows us to see things from a more objective perspective, which will enable us to be more compassionate toward ourselves and others.
- Detachment gives us the inner strength to face challenges and overcome obstacles.

Common Mistakes
- Involvement is about the process, not the result. People are looking for the result they will gain; once they understand the gain, they will become more involved. However, total involvement is about being true to the process, and if we are sincere, the results will come.
- Students and working professionals have too much exposure to social media and OTT shows. Billions of

dollars are paid to these marketing professionals to keep everyone engaged on these platforms. What started as entertainment has now become an obsession. The problem is it takes away your time of focus and involvement to do something productive
- Multitasking is not for everyone. Some yogis, known as *Das avatars*, can follow ten chains of thoughts together. Unless you reach that level, please do one thing at a time.
- There is no line to draw between involvement and attachment. Start with detachment and then get involved.

❝ Success Tip

Be like a volunteer

A volunteer is someone who says yes to life. They are open to accepting new ideas and opportunities and continue to be devoted to the task that has been provided to them. They understand the intelligence of devotion and, therefore, can leap beyond the physiological barriers of willpower and mental concentration. They do everything with joy and purpose without attaching themselves too much to the results. They leave everything in the hands of their devotion and stay true to the process.

Next time you approach something new, act like a volunteer and stay devoted to the process. A volunteer is only attached to the process; therefore, the end results in worldly success do not bind them in any manner.

CHAPTER 12

TRADE YOUR BEST FRIENDS FOR BOOKS

THIS ONE is the closest to my heart, so close that I wrote an entire book about it. My first book, *Books, Ideas & You*, discussed creating wealth and happiness through the world of books.

I became successful because I stayed away from the world of books, said no one. If there is one thing common among all the successful people in this world, it is the fact that they embraced the world of books. They are all avid readers who know how to use what they have learned in books. In their interviews or videos, you would see in the background a YouTube milestone prize in gold/silver; I am kidding. You would notice an almirah full of books.

If you are reading or listening to this book, I can safely imagine you are not allergic to them. If you are already on the path of a reader, you will notice that it is filled with new experiences, ideas, knowledge, anecdotes, principles, and life lessons. However, wherever I go, I hear about how young minds are moving away from books; I believe that problem is now just with the youth.

A recent research showed that the average human attention

span decreased from twelve seconds in 2000 to eight seconds in 2018. According to this study by Microsoft, the rising popularity of smartphones, mobile data, messaging apps, and social media is the cause behind falling attention rates. Therefore, it's important to remember the potential long-term benefits you would derive once you continue becoming a reader. Some of these benefits could be:

1. **An insight into the unknown:** There is so much about this world that we do not know. The yogic sciences often encourage us to identify ourselves with what is unknown. That's because if we keep our focus on what we already know, there would be no passion to explore the unknown. We all have such people whose shoe size exceeds their IQ levels, but they portray it as if they know everything. I feel sad to see people arguing on any topic with the vague knowledge they get through messages circulating on Facebook and WhatsApp. So, to know the truth or facts about anything, we must explore the world of books. This is not to win an argument on social media with our friends but to understand that the argument itself is not worth it.

2. **An answer to every Question:** I did a quick search online and found about forty thousand books on health, so there is no shortage of knowledge on any topic if we are willing to see it. If we want to become wealthy, there is a book; if we want to become creative, there is a book; if we want to become a home chef, there is a book; if we want to embrace spirituality, there is a book, if we want to know about black holes there is a book, if we want to become a stock market trader there is a book, if we want to become a better husband, there is a book (not sure if anyone would be buying), even if we want to become the next Sharukh

Khan there is a book. Please get my point; any question that comes to your mind shall be answered through the world of books.

3. **A new perspective:** Many people are experts at creating a problem from a solution. Do one thing: please watch a video on health and fitness by some famous health experts on YouTube. Now read the comments below that video; we will read hundreds of comments from people on why this is impossible for them due to money, time, or networking issues. If the expert is saying we need to eat 300 grams of cottage cheese (paneer) every day to meet our protein requirements and let's say that costs hundred, instead of figuring out where to earn that three thousand (hundred rupees X Thirty) extra in a month, people are making an excuse to stay unhealthy. We must change our emotional and mental inputs to change our perspective, and there is no better positive influence than the world of books. An underlying message that we would receive in the world of books is what Napoleon Hill said, "Every adversity, every failure, every heartache carries with it the seed of an equal or greater benefit."

4. **A dose of imagination:** Most know only what we were taught in schools and colleges. We cramped it up to get good grades. But there is an entire world beyond academic knowledge, where we start with our imagination. Albert Einstein puts it best when he says: "Logic will get you from A to B; imagination will take you everywhere." Today, we are wandering in our schools, colleges, and workspaces. We are not getting creative ideas, which has everything to do with the content we feed our minds. A

new idea comes from the permutations and combinations of existing information in our head. However, suppose most of our time goes into watching Big Boss, MTV Splits Villa, and Superhero movies, with all due respect to these serials and films. In that case, we are not giving our mind anything productive to work on. Maybe we would imagine a superhero whose special powers are bitching about people, but what good is that.

5. **Return on Investment of Time:** The book *Think & Grow Rich* by Napolean Hill is the single most significant reason why we should all be invested in the ideas of books. The book, released in 1930, is culmination of twenty years of hard work by the author, who interviewed five hundred of the most successful people on this planet and wrote about their success habits. All this combined means over ten thousand years of experience culminated into a 3-hour book. This should be enough to blow our mind and get the focus back on reading.

6. **Other people's experiences:** We grow in life as we learn with age through our experiences. Learning with age is an individual phenomenon and irreplaceable. We could look back and learn from our past experiences to prepare for the future. However, we often forget that we can acquire knowledge in two ways.
   - Our own experiences
   - Other people's experiences

When we read books, we learn from other people's experiences. Books contain knowledge acquired by experiments and understanding of some of the most remarkable men and women who have walked this planet. For example, when we study physics in schools and colleges, we acquire knowledge from hundreds of the most outstanding scientists over thousands of years. Reading books of good writers is like conversing with the wisest people of the world who authored these books.

An Advice for Students

Consider this, 95% of the students today who graduate have absolutely no idea in which direction they would take their careers. Well, I may be wrong in my assessment of that number; it may be higher.

The school and universities today offer great advice on technical parameters, they do very little to enhance the life skills for our students. The government of the day has been taking great strides in this direction but here are certain things which the students can do themselves:

- **Self Help Books for Curriculum** – Just like you have your books to study for your school and college exams, consider having some great books for your personal curriculum. Not just read these books but engage with them. These books should especially focus on life skills like communication, goal setting, emotional intelligence, stress management, creative thinking, interpersonal relationships, decision making and many more.

- **E-Books & Audiobooks** – Today the world has expanded rapidly in terms of opportunities available for users to choose their preferred way for studying. Your phone is the biggest university for you, only if you are willing to use it aptly.

- **Engage in Social & Community Building Platforms** –

Joining a local community platform like the Toastmasters club or Book club could go a long way in your personal as well as professional growth. These community clubs provide the perfect setting for you to practice in a safe environment and get feedback from folks who are neutral and do not have any hidden agenda.

- **Speak with Industry Experts** – Experts today are largely willing to share their knowledge and experiences for free, simply because they know that spreading knowledge is necessary for uplifting the collective consciousness of this world. Students must make use of this opportunity. One hour of your exchange with these experts is equivalent to hours of book reading.

An Advice for Professionals

Most of the working professionals spend years of their professional career not investing enough time in the world of books. They later wonder why some of their colleagues seem to be surpassing them in the organizational hierarchy. Most of these professionals cannot even recollect last time they picked up a proper book to read. If you would ask them the reason, they would come back with excuses like; not having enough time, not having any interest, too much hard work, not able to decide which books to read etc. While the excuses can pile on, however if you are someone who is willing to look beyond this pile of excuses, then here is some advice for you:

- **Industry Expert:** Becoming an expert in your industry is not rocket science, all it takes for you to pick up the top 50 books which are written by experts in your industry. If you can read a book in a week then after a year you would be in top 4% of experts in your industry.

The only question is are you willing to do this grind?

- **Communication is Key:** Research has shown that two people starting together a company at a same level, but, the person with better communication skillset is likely to move ahead. So even if you claim that you have limited time to give in for improving all your skillset, at least read those books which help improve your communication skills.

- **Mobile University:** If you are not a big fan of reading books, maybe you could invest in listening to some of the audiobooks. For me one of the most profound investments of time has been listening to these audiobooks while commuting to and from office. Those 2-3 hours of investment which you do on a daily basis would start showing its impact over a period of time.

- **Having a Mentor:** Getting a mentor who is powerhouse of books is a great way to learn. The mentor would open the window of opportunities for you to consider through the world of books which he had been though over last many years. So even if you do not invest too much time reading yourself, have someone who passes on that knowledge through his experience and expertise.

- **Professional Allies:** You may not be someone who is interested too much in reading, but you could always learn from those friends and acquaintances who actually are interested. Share your thoughts, ideas and experiences with them. Let them enrich those experiences through their wealth of knowledge.

Common Mistakes

- Sometimes we may be overwhelmed by the task and cannot imagine ourselves reading the entire book. We must start small even if we can read a few pages daily, that's great.
- Losing track of the book's sequence and reading again to understand where we left off. That's just being naïve. It's like remembering our girlfriend's pet's birthday but forgetting our wife's; we remember what interests us.
- We may be procrastinating about when to read the next chapter or the book. Schedule reading as part of our daily routine, early morning or late night because that's when the distraction is minimal.
- Not finding enough value in the reading habit, so giving up too early. Everything takes time, so give ourselves that time to adopt this new habit.
- Not knowing how to make the most of the learnings from books. Read the success tip below.
- If we don't find the nonfiction books interesting enough, start with the fictional ones and slowly move towards those books with stories and lessons, like books by Robin Sharma, that would fire our curiosity.
- Not being able to decide which books to read. In this case, read those books that provide insights and lessons connected to our goals. These could be about business, health, money, or relationships. Don't read books just for entertainment; there is more to them.

Success Tip

Too many people read books but never really take away those learnings into their practical world. Reading a book once and never returning to it is like only scratching the surface. There is an art behind making the most out of learning from anywhere, including the world of books; here is some advice:

1. **Identify your purpose or goal for reading:** To learn from reading, you must understand why you're reading in the first place. If you figure out the objective, it will keep you away from less helpful information, like books with juicy headlines and covers, and orient you towards beneficial details. Also, your objective will impact your reading decisions, so you don't read mindlessly, which can be tempting.

2. **Engage with book by making mental connections:** Science is pretty straightforward: The more neuro connections you make between pieces of information in your brain, the better you remember it. Reading should be more like a conversation than a lecture. Therefore, it's like engaging in a silent dialogue with the author.

3. **Visualize and Imagine:** Creative visualization is a technique that uses imagination to create and visualize scenarios in your mind. By using visualization techniques, you create a mental picture of something and then focus on that image for a certain period of time, thinking as if it's already happened. Next time you read a book and

come across an idea, make sure you use that idea as a platform to imagine that it has already been successfully implemented.

4. **Take Action!:** Always remember that when people say that knowledge is power, they tell you an incomplete truth: Knowledge is potential power, and applied knowledge is power. Therefore, it's essential to ask yourself the following question each time you have finished a book, *'What are some of the things I have learned from this book, and how many of these am I willing to apply to my practical life?'*

5. **Process, analyze and revisit:** Revisiting your favorite passages over time is a great way to keep a book's most important parts alive. This allows you to enjoy a book long after you finish it and apply its lessons as new opportunities and insights arise.

CHAPTER 13

CREATE A SOCIAL MEDIA BRAND FOR YOURSELF

I GENERALLY come across three kinds of people on social media platforms: Those who typically know what they are doing, the second type who have no idea how this process works, then there is a third kind who knows how to make destructive use of these platforms to serve their agendas. You would see these people arguing about who is more popular: Shahrukh, Salman, Virat, or Dhoni. These are the ones that take every comment to heart and love to give it back to the world. These people think that Modi Ji will not win the next set of elections if they don't make any political posts or comment on other political posts. These are also the ones that often disguise or shield themselves behind social media and use derogatory remarks against anyone and everyone who disagrees with their line of thinking. Please take my advice: Don't be the third kind.

We all know how powerful social media and technology, in general, have become. One of the most amazing books on the subject is *Tools and Weapons* by Brad Smith and Carol Ann Browne. Perhaps more than any industry leader, Brad Smith (Microsoft's president) understands that technology is a double-edged sword, unleashing incredible opportunity but raising profound questions about democracy, civil liberties, the future of work, and international relations. The core belief of the book is that when your technology changes the world, you bear a responsibility to help address the world you have helped create. How many of us are willing to take up that responsibility? How many of us care that everything we write on social media platforms has a bearing on us, our friends, and the world? The digital footprint that we create will stay there forever and determine how the world perceives us. The same people who belittle each other can unite to transform this world for good.

You may skip this chapter if you are already among the first kind of people who are making fantastic use of social media platforms and technology. But if you are one of those figuring stuff out, let's read the inspiring story of Milkuri Gangavva.

Milkuri Gangavva is no less than a star, with millions watching her videos on the YouTube channel, My Village Show (MVS). From acting in funny sketches to interviewing celebrities, Gangavva has been stealing the hearts of millions on the internet, even the likes of actors Kajal Aggarwal and Vijay Deverakonda. Born in the small village of Lambadipally in Telangana, she dropped out of school to become a daily wager. It was only in 2016 that the 60-year-old's son-in-law, Srikanth Sriram, asked her to make guest appearances in his funny sketches for his YouTube channel. The show addressed issues faced by the rural population with a tinge of humor. With her comic timing and natural acting skills, Gangavva quickly became a YouTube sensation. She even went on to act in several Telugu movies like *iSmart Shankar* (2019) and *Mallesham* (2019).

Are you one of those who think our resources are limited

in terms of time, money, and network? The best part about creating a brand online is that we need minimum resources. All we need is a smartphone that should not be smarter than us; what I mean is before we go about this business, do some research on the subject, see what brand identity we want to create, which stream of messaging we want to use, i.e., written posts or videos or podcasts. Maybe we can start by reading some of these golden rules.

Golden Rules!

Figure 4: 7 Golden rules of Personal Branding

Golden Rule 1 – Starting with the end in mind means having our end objective clear regarding what we are trying to achieve. If we want to become a yoga instructor, post videos and images that support that goal; don't add commentary on world issues. Many people are confused about their end objective and give mixed messages through their profiles. Many travel and food vloggers are doing a great job in this domain.

Golden Rule 2 – Everyone is selling something; being a seller is not the problem, but whatever we sell should add value to the audience. It's our job to communicate how the service or product would offer that value by educating the audience. Merely trying to sell or rake up our follower's numbers would not serve our purpose in the long run.

Golden Rule 3 – Being cool does not mean wearing a hoody. It means we should come across as easygoing and fun-loving to the audience. Our audience should not be intimidated by our strong views on the subject. There is nothing wrong with being opinionated, just don't be a hardliner. Leave your mind open to new ideas and opinions which you would anyways receive through comments. The engagement is better when we are connected with the audience.

Golden Rule 4 – Paying attention means understanding what the audience wants and changing our theme, methodology, and execution-style to match the requirements.

Golden Rule 5 – Unless we are passionate about whatever we discuss, we are unlikely to catch people's attention. People can tell if we are not authentic and making things up.

Golden Rule 6 – As the saying goes, to bleed less on the field, we must sweat more in the training. Practicing our videos, speeches, and content always helps. Practice also means researching our content thoroughly before posting.

Golden Rule 7 – People would not pay attention unless they know our story. Always have a good story to tell from your life that can appeal to and connect with the audience.

Here are some additional technical tips:

- **Use Relevant Hashtags:** Hashtags are a great way to get our content seen by more people. When we use appropriate hashtags, our posts will show up in search results for those hashtags.
- **Run Contests and Giveaways:** These are great ways to generate excitement and engagement around our brand and attract new followers.
- **Partner with Other Brands:** Partnering with other brands is a great way to reach a new audience and grow our brand. Partner with brands that are in your industry, or that share your target audience.
- **Attend Industry Events:** Attending industry events is a great way to meet new people and learn about trends. We can also use these events to network and promote our brand.
- **Be Patient:** Building a solid social media brand takes time. So, don't get discouraged if you don't see results overnight. Keep posting great content, engaging with your followers, and using social media analytics to track your progress.
- **Define Our Goals:** First, let's clarify our objectives for using social media. Are we looking to showcase our academic achievements, connect with other students and professionals, build a personal brand, or something else? Understanding our goals will guide our strategy.
- **Choose Our Platforms:** Different social media platforms cater to different audiences and content types. As a student and young professional, you might consider platforms like LinkedIn for professional networking, Twitter for sharing thoughts and ideas, Instagram for visual content, and possibly TikTok or YouTube for more creative and engaging content. The same type of content does not

work everywhere.
- **Create a Consistent Brand Identity:** Our brand identity is how we want to be perceived by our audience. It includes our profile picture, username, bio, and overall visual style. Use a professional-looking photo and a username that aligns with the brand. Hire a marketing partner to build this identity.
- **Develop a Content Strategy:** Decide on the type of content you want to create and share. It could include academic achievements, personal experiences, industry-related insights, tips for other students and young professionals, and anything else that aligns with the goals and interests. Again, work with the marketing partner on this strategy.
- **Post Regularly and Engage:** Consistency is vital on social media. Try to post regularly, but don't sacrifice quality for quantity. Engage with the audience by responding to comments and messages and participating in relevant discussions to grow the network.
- **Showcase Your Skills:** As a student and young professional, you offer unique skills and knowledge. Share your achievements, projects, and experiences, highlighting your expertise and dedication.
- **Network and Collaborate:** Connect with other students, young professionals, and industry influencers in your field. Engaging with others by collaborating on projects or content can help expand your reach and build valuable connections.
- **Analyze and Adapt:** Monitor your social media metrics to understand what content resonates best with your audience. Use insights to adapt your strategy and optimize your content for better engagement.

Common Mistakes
- Thinking that personal branding is only for sales people or influencers, it is for everyone because everyone is a brand trying to sell something.
- Choosing a medium with which we are not too comfortable, learn to adapt, learn, and transform.
- Procrastinating on our next move. Plan for the next five moves.
- Not finding enough value in this journey. Remember, all good things take time.

❝ Success Tip

The only strategy that really works in creating a personal brand is for you to learn, adapt and be consistent in your messaging. If you are lost in your abyss, the world will forget about you. You need to be out there for the world to remind you that you not only exist but also matter!

People want to connect with those people who are authentic. So, in general one thing that always works is when you relate things to your life story, your failures, your success stories, your family values, your beliefs, your travel journey. Sharing inspiring videos and stories of others is great, you may get the likes, but strong connections only build when you can put yourself out there without any shame or judgements.

CHAPTER 14

RESERVE THE COMPLAINS & CRITICISM FOR YOURSELF

I AM sure you have heard of this children's story named, 'Thomas and his disappearing day'. If you haven't, then here is the crux:

One day, Thomas woke up in a grumpy mood. He first said, "I don't want to brush my teeth." And suddenly, right before his eyes, his toothbrush disappeared! Thomas thought that was strange, but he was happy he wouldn't have to brush his teeth.

At breakfast, Thomas whined about his cold and sticky porridge. Suddenly, his porridge vanished, too!

Thomas' friend Gordon came out to play, but Gordon wanted to go fishing instead of tag, so Thomas groaned about his friend. "Gordon, you never want to play what I want," he said. As quickly as you can blink your eye, Gordon was gone.

By lunchtime, Thomas was hungry and slightly bored with playing alone. He went inside and said to his mother in a whiny voice, "I have nothing to do. And I am so hungry! A good mother would have my lunch made already, wouldn't she?" Then, in a flash, Thomas' mother was gone too.

Thomas searched the kitchen for something to eat. When

he couldn't reach the shelves in the pantry, he grumbled that the food had been stored too high up. Then Thomas looked in the fridge and muttered that it had no fun food. Suddenly, everything was empty in the cupboards and fridge!

"All there's left for me to do is play with my toys, but they are all so old and boring." And as soon as he said that, all Thomas' toys floated up and away out the window.

Then Thomas heard the house creaking and echoing. It seemed to say, "You should stop complaining."

Feeling sorry for himself, Thomas said in his saddest voice, "Even the house is bothering me." And before he could take back what he had said, the house was gone, too.

Thomas found himself sitting on the lawn and began to cry. Soon, his pet cat, Morris, came and rubbed up against him. "Silly cat," said Thomas. "You want me to pet you? How selfish can you be? I have all these problems, and you want attention. If only I could have a sensible pet instead."

And what do you think happened next? That's right. Thomas' cat disappeared too.

When Thomas' father came home for supper, he found a lonely, hungry, thirsty, and uncomfortable little boy sitting in an empty yard.

"Daddy," said Thomas, "I'm so sorry for all my whining. All day, whenever I complained, things just disappeared. From now on, I will try to be thankful for all I have instead of complaining."

Then, just as quickly as everything had gone, it reappeared. Thomas' mother, friend, house, and cat were all back again.

Luckily for us, things don't disappear in front of us the moment we complain about them. But take a moment to reverse our lives for a few days, as far back as our memory can serve, and try to remember the times we have complained about. Maybe that dinner was not cooked well, that cab that didn't come on time, maybe our sports team lost again, or perhaps that friend who stole our partner. (fine your partner)

As we recollect those moments, also reflect on the emotions we were experiencing like anger, frustration, dejection, despise, and many more. The whole experience was rather unpleasant for us and for everyone around us.

Why is criticism or complaint self-destructive?

- **Negative emotions:** When we complain or criticize, we are focusing on the negative aspects of a situation, which may become our second nature and affect other aspects of our life. We then tend to always see the glass half empty. I don't care if the glass is half-empty or half-filled as long as I get to drink that water, but you get my point.
- **Relationship crisis:** When we complain or criticize, we essentially put someone or something down. Complaining about your wife's cooking can damage relationships and make you sleep without food.
- **Unproductive:** When we complain or criticize, we do nothing to solve the problem. If anything, we are making it worse since now we have two problems to solve: The one that existed and our peace of mind.
- **Contagious:** We have all had that teacher or manager who goes out of their way to find our mistakes as if it's their life's purpose. We wonder if it gives them some sadistic pleasure or maybe it helps them digest their food. Either way, it leaves a bad taste in the mouth, and I only want you to promise that you shall not be that teacher or manager when you are put into that role. There are enough scientific studies to suggest that those teachers who encourage their children to achieve more are likely

to see better results at the end of the year. There have been miraculous turnaround stories showing us the power of faith and belief. The challenge is that only a few teachers or managers have a classroom or a cabin where criticism does not enter. It's a special place indeed!

So, what shall you do instead of complaining or criticizing?

Show some Gratitude-
Countless studies have shown that gratitude can bring various physical, psychological, emotional, and social benefits. It helps us appreciate all the positive elements of our lives and the people in it. While it might not be a panacea or cure-all for everything, gratitude can help keep us grounded and positive, particularly in times of uncertainty. Many of us are familiar with feelings of dissatisfaction – we feel that our lives are incomplete and lacking in the things we crave. At such times, it's easy to compare ourselves to the idyllic-seeming lives of others and judge ourself to be lacking. The simple practice of gratitude can help alleviate these feelings. The rule is simple: If we want more beautiful situations and people in our life, show appreciation to the ones that exist.

1) Constructive Criticism-
   This has become a bit of a cliché, and I understand it's often challenging to be both constructive and critical simultaneously. The simple way to overcome this is to delay when we think it's time to criticize. Never rush into these things, especially when we are angry. Imagine how the situation would play out in our head. Only if the outcome is coming out as a win-win should we go ahead.

Planning ahead of these discussions helps channelize our emotions.

2) Appreciate Others-
A little appreciation goes a long way; thus, it has been named one of the most powerful communication tools. Next time you speak with someone, add a sentence or two appreciating something different about them. It could be their dressing style, vocabulary, sense of confidence, or some creative art they practice, like music, painting, etc. For leaders, they must personalize these appreciations. This means rather than sending general emails to the team mentioning, 'Great Job, Team, appreciate your efforts!' highlight specific people to appreciate and specify the reason for your appreciation. For example, 'Highly Appreciate Arun for taking additional responsibilities on this project.' Also, do not be stingy in your gratitude to others; be wholehearted and unconditional.

3) Listen Carefully, respond rather than react-
Listening is critical in any environment. We would be amazed if we allowed people to speak and express themselves; we would become one of the most excellent communicators in their eyes. I only speak in front of people I meet for the first time when I ask questions. Let them run wild with their talk, absorb everything calmly. Most people are impulsive by nature; they are itching to speak, so much so that they often do not even allow the other person to complete it. We have all experienced such people; you feel like putting your toe in their mouths.

4) Being Genuine – In Smile, Compliments, Interests and Admission-
   I could not teach this to anyone; it's reflected in one's character. Each smile or encouragement we give our friends or co-workers should come from the heart. It should not look like we are making something up to impress another person. A genuine smile and encouragement would create an authentic connection. At the same time, when we understand that we have sinned, be quick and sincere in our apology. It's important to realize that the other person can quickly gauge if we are not genuine in our approach.

Common Mistakes

- People are not even conscious when they criticize someone or complain about something; for them, it's a daily affair. Please don't be one of those people.
- Never run away from genuine criticism; please don't take this learning as an excuse. Our job is not to ensure everyone likes you; please do what's best for others.
- Taking greater responsibility for ourselves means giving our best shot at achieving the goal; it does not mean pushing ourselves to the point where you break. Sometimes, we over-criticize ourselves and, in the process, create doubt about whether we are worthy of this achievement.
- Do not go overboard as well in your appreciation; we could become a slot machine throwing away products for free.

Success Tip

The best thing I did for myself was get a gratitude journal. It gave me a window to channel my emotions and a dose of everyday realizations about how lucky I was that life had offered me so much.

While regular journaling has been proven to improve your well-being, jotting down all the things you are grateful for can take the experience to a whole new level. Keeping a gratitude journal is easy, and on the most superficial level, it involves noting what you are grateful for that day. You can decide how long your list is each day and how much detail you want to go into. The great thing is that it's an easy habit to form, and after a while, you are left with a collection of inspiring material to look back on when you are in need. You can write about:

- Someone you're glad to have in your life.
- Your favorite part of the day.
- Positive news or something that made you smile.
- A favorite song or painting.
- A gift you've recently received.
- Lesson learned.
- Favorite place in the local area.
- A recent compliment.
- Someone who inspired you.

- A challenge you overcame recently.
- What you love about the place you live in.
- A hobby you have.
- Something you love about your work.
- One thing you adore about your body.
- A friend who gives you the best advice.
- Someone who gives you support.
- Your favorite cafe or restaurant.
- One thing you're incredibly proud of.

Today, I am filled with gratitude for you, the reader of this book. Your interest and engagement in this topic are truly appreciated.

CHAPTER 15

BECAUSE GIVERS ALWAYS WIN IN THE END

KARAMBIR SINGH Kang was the Taj Mumbai's General Manager when the Mumbai Terrorist attacks broke out. He was at another location, but he immediately returned to the hotel to guide evacuations. Kang led hundreds of guests safely, ensuring they found escape routes amidst chaos and danger. He was the last person to leave the hotel, demonstrating extraordinary courage and commitment. Tragically, Kang's wife and two children lost their lives during the terror attacks.

I sometimes wonder how do you create such people who are willing to sacrifice their lives in the line of duty to protect their clients. Actually, you cannot create such people; you create an ecosystem which creates such people. That is why TATA is such a unique business model in the Indian context that every Indian should read and be aware of.

The heroic response by employees of Mumbai's landmark Taj Hotel during the 26/11 terror attacks is now a case study at Harvard Business School. The study focuses on the staff's selfless service to its customers and how they went beyond their call of duty to save lives.

"Not even the senior managers could explain the behavior

of these employees," HBS professor Deshpande is quoted as saying. Deshpande said, even though the employees "knew all the back exits" in the hotel and could have quickly fled the building, some stayed back to help the guests. "The natural human instinct would be to flee. These are people who instinctively did the right thing. And in the process, some of them, unfortunately, gave their lives to save guests."

A way to explain this is perhaps that TATA rewards employees who are faithful givers in the sense that they keep customers first at all costs. TATA knows that those values would create long-term benefits for the company. Givers don't always win but are more successful in the long run. It means you may lose a battle or two but would undoubtedly win the war. So, who is a giver, and how do they think?

1. The Giver Mindset

Givers genuinely seek to help others without expecting anything in return. They focus on what others need from them and are generous with their time, knowledge, energy, skills, and interactions. It's not just about donating money or volunteering; it's about positively impacting others' lives. Therefore, a giver is a salesman who would only sell to a customer if they think that product or service would add value to their lives; a giver is that nurturing parent who does not vent out their frustration but instead cares to explain to a child if that child commits a mistake, a giver is that teacher who makes an effort to teach beyond what is prescribed in the school curriculum, a giver is also that professional or student who stays late in office or college to help colleagues/students in solving their problems.

Now, you might wonder if it makes practical sense for anyone to go beyond their expected behaviors and support others. Is it financially viable for that salesman? Wouldn't it affect their sales numbers? You might also wonder, what if I give, give, and give and get nothing in return? Before we diagnose this problem, let's look at what a taker's mindset represents.

2. The Taker Mindset

Takers prioritize their interests above all else. They aim to extract as much as possible from interactions while contributing as little. A taker is that salesman who wants to achieve that monthly target at any cost, that student who wants to get the desired result in the examination without thinking about adding value to their life, that professional who wants to succeed as a manager without showing the slightest compassion for their team members.

But you see, human beings do not operate that way. Anyone who thinks only for themselves is often left alone by their friends and loved ones to enjoy the benefits. You would have heard that some people are so rich that all they have is money. Research shows that people envy successful takers and look for ways to knock them down a notch. Takers' self-centered approach can alienate them, leading to a lack of support and potential backlash.

Even wealth experts are against these takers. Compared to givers, takers earn fourteen per cent less money on average. Additionally, takers face a higher risk of becoming victims of crimes and are perceived as less powerful and dominant. Their short-term gains may come at a significant cost.

Now, this chapter would be incomplete without mentioning the most famous book on the subject, *Give & Take* by Adam Grant. Grant argues that givers are likelier to be promoted, earn higher salaries, and have more fulfilling relationships. This is because givers build strong networks of relationships, create a positive reputation, and are seen as more trustworthy and competent. Let's break these three things down:

- Givers build strong relationships-
  When we help others, they are more likely to help us. This creates a web of interconnected relationships that can benefit us in many ways. For example, self-reflect on our relationship with our lover or spouse. A relationship is like building a water reservoir; we can throw in a bucket or pull some out. If we like to give more, we would continue to throw in those buckets; if we were a taker, we would continue to pull out the buckets. In a relationship, if both are takers, the reservoir becomes empty soon enough, and that's where the trouble starts. Givers build strong relationships at home, work, and in this world.

- Givers create a positive reputation-
  As the story above describes, TATA is often used as a synonym for trust. It hasn't happened overnight. When people think of trust, they usually associate it with reliability, confidence, and faith in someone or something. The Tata Group, founded by Jamshedji Tata, has trust in its DNA. Ethical decision-making, compassion towards employees, nation-first strategy, customer-centric approach, and the philanthropic efforts of the Tata Trusts have certainly contributed to building trust in the hearts and minds of the people of the group. People are more likely to trust and respect those who are generous with their time and resources. This can lead to opportunities that would not be available to takers. Therefore, givers are more likely to be given preferential treatment by employers, clients, and

colleagues. This means more salary hikes, bigger chunks of the business, and higher profits.

- Givers are seen as more competent-
People are more likely to believe that givers are capable and knowledgeable. This can lead to promotions and higher salaries. For example, givers are likelier to be seen as leaders and mentors.

Of course, there are also some risks associated with being a giver. For example, givers can be taken advantage of by takers. However, if we are strategic about giving, we can minimize these risks and reap the many benefits of being a giver. Here is how:

- Give with intention - Don't just give for the sake of giving. Give to create a positive impact on the situation or the person.
- Be selective about who you give to - Not all takers are created equal. Some takers are more likely to take advantage of you than others. Be selective about who you give to and be prepared to walk away from those not worthy of your time and resources.
- Set boundaries - It's important to set boundaries when we are giving. Don't be afraid to say no when feeling overwhelmed or exploited.
- Generosity in Small Acts - Begin with small acts of kindness. Hold the door for someone, offer a genuine compliment, or lend a helping hand. Practice random acts of kindness without expecting anything in return.
- Networking with a Giving Mindset - When networking or building relationships, focus on what we can offer rather

than gain. Introduce people to each other, share resources, and actively listen to their needs.
- Seek Opportunities to Help - Volunteer your time or skills. Find causes or organizations that resonate with you. Mentor someone—whether it's a colleague, student, or friend.
- Celebrate Others' Success - Instead of feeling envious, celebrate when others achieve their goals. Acknowledge their accomplishments genuinely.
- Learn from Givers Around You - Observe people who embody the giver mindset. What do they do differently? Seek inspiration from role models like Warren Buffett, Bill Gates, or local community leaders.

Common Mistakes

- Having a short-term mindset: If we don't think about the long term, we will be caught with the idea that givers lose in the short term because they often do.
- Remember that time when we had revenge on our mind? Takers tend to have that mindset of settling scores. If we get lost in this game of taking revenge for everything that has gone wrong with us, we will lose out on precious time for building what we wanted to create. The rule is to forgive but never forget. Forgive for our peace, but never forget so that we don't make the same mistake again.
- Keeping track of how much we have given is the most common mistake, especially when fighting with our loved ones. We constantly remind them of the time when we were there for them, which takes away the grace and purity of the situation and puts us in the category of a taker from

a giver. Stay humble, and don't keep track!
- Some battles are best left alone. A giver does not have time to prove to others that they are a giver. When confronted with minor issues, givers tap out to save relationships.

❝ Success Tip

A giver is usually a character trait rather than a personality one. The difference is that either you have it or you don't. A character is a set of values that define your behavior, and if you want to alter your behavior, you must work on your values. Creating a superficial image of a giver won't help; people will be able to see through that image in the long run.

Therefore, if you want to cultivate the values of the giver, you must work on the principles first. Go back to the time of your life when you were a true giver and reflect on what prompted that behavior. It could be a donation drive you participated in, it could be an NGO you supported, it could be a blind person you helped on the road, it could be a fellow student you helped, or it could be a client you didn't charge because they didn't have the resources to pay. Please pick up the pieces of that behavior and make it your standard behavior. Small changes in this direction could significantly impact in the long run.

CHAPTER 16

DO NOT ROMANTICIZE WITH THE ROMANCE

WHEN WE think of romance, we think of Shahrukh Khan and the larger-than-life college romances in the Karan Johar movies, but we all know real life is very different.

Let me take you back to my college days. Many friends from my MBA college knew the art of managing their romances with their studies; it's not easy. If you spoke with them, they would tell you that when they first met their partners, they found themselves spending more time together and started neglecting their academic responsibilities. Therefore, the first semester was gone in an instant.

Maybe the call from their parents or self-realization caught up with them, jolted them and made their return from their dreamy world. Maybe they implemented a study schedule or designated "no-distraction" zones and communicated openly about their academic goals; who knows? I never interviewed to find out. Today, most of them are married and have a beautiful and healthy life together. There were, of course, a few whose relationships expired when college ended; my best guess is that they had a memorandum of understanding. Then there were the likes of me, who tragically wasted an entire year searching for a girlfriend. The precious time that should have been spent on completing my assignments and studying for my exams was given away in search of romance. I have no shame in accepting this because I was hoping you could learn from my mistakes and not commit them yourself. It's rightly said that you don't put your hand in the fire to check if it's hot.

While college romance can be exciting, students should avoid romanticizing the idea of romance at the expense of their academic pursuits. Unrealistic expectations, excessive time spent with a partner, and emotional dependency can hinder academic performance and personal growth.

Why do people go overboard?

For many students, college represents a newfound sense of freedom and independence, providing fertile ground for romantic exploration. The proximity of peers, shared interests, and vibrant social scenes often facilitate the formation of romantic connections. Moreover, the emotional support and companionship offered by romantic partners can be exceptionally comforting during the transition to adulthood. Numerous studies have explored the relationship between romantic involvement and academic achievement among college students.

A study published in the *Journal of Youth and Adolescence* found that while romantic relationships can positively affect emotional well-being, they can also detract from academic focus and time management if not balanced effectively. Another study published in the *Journal of Social and Personal Relationships* highlighted the importance of maintaining individual identity and autonomy within romantic partnerships to prevent academic interference. Dr. Emily Richards, a psychologist specializing in adolescent development, emphasizes the significance of setting boundaries and prioritizing self-care in college relationships. Dr. Richards states, "Maintaining a healthy balance between romance and studies requires open communication, time management skills, and a commitment to personal growth. Students should prioritize their academic goals while nurturing their relationships in a way that enhances, rather than detracts from, their overall well-being."

So, what should we do?

Are you wondering if I should stop watching Karan Johar movies? Should I ignore my physical, emotional, and sometimes financial needs (if one partner is wealthy)? First of all, do not get too emotional and dramatic, and look at the suggestions below objectively:

- **Prioritize Self-Care:** Love yourself first; this rule has no replacement. Yes, we all need companionship and emotional support but do not compromise on your desires. Indeed, it would be best if you never lost sight of your goals, like getting an A grade, which I never got.
- **Choose Wisely:** Seek stable relationships that uplift and inspire you to achieve something together. Be with someone who has your best interest in mind. Avoid toxic dynamics that drain your energy. Don't jump on the first opportunity for companionship, and certainly don't stay in a place where you are no longer valued.
- **Time Management:** Allocate time for both studies and love. Set boundaries to prevent one from overshadowing the other. Learn from my MBA friends, not from me.
- **Stay Focused:** In life, we are asked by our teachers to concentrate and stay focused, but no one teaches us how. These three techniques would certainly help:
    o Meditation - Sitting alone and meditating first thing

in the morning would help channel your energy and keep you focused on your goal.
- o Remember your why – Reminding yourself daily as to why you are doing what you are doing keeps you on track.
- o Productivity hacks – The chapter on productivity hacks below would help you obtain maximum output from minimum input.

Now, returning to movies, you are not Raj or Simran, and I am not your Amrish Puri, who is standing in the way of your blossoming romance. But if we would like to think that our romance is unique and one of a kind, then be my guest and turn this world upside down for her as Manoj Kumar Sharma did in the movie *12th Fail*. I am here to remind you that don't spend all your time and energy searching for a romantic relationship; let it happen naturally. Unfortunately, people think that being in a relationship is a status symbol, and not being in one makes one weak, socially awkward, and basically a loser. NOPE: Let's put our hand on our heart and remind ourselves that I am a complete life.

Common Mistakes
- Do not mistake love for romance; if we seek love as an emotion, we can always become loving to express that feeling towards others. Being in love does not require another person and certainly doesn't apply only to partners.
- Being in a relationship is never a problem; the trouble starts when we build our life around it, keeping it at the center.
- A lot of students become angry or depressed if a romance does not work out; nothing can be more unfortunate than

that. Remember what SRK said at the start of *KKHH*: We love only once, but later, he retracted his words and fell in love again.
- Not seeking help when we need it the most, not from some Love Guru but rather from someone sensible enough who knows us well.

> ## Success Tip

Whatever you try to run away from will follow you even more. Don't try to avoid the subject of love and romance; instead, look for a stable relationship.

Imagine and write down the qualities you would want to see in your life partner, how that person would look, how they would talk, how they would behave, what character traits would stand out, and even what kind of pets they like. The idea is to manifest that person into your life, and once you have them, never let go.

CHAPTER 17

PRODUCTIVITY HACKS MASTER THEM

EUGENE PAULY was an unassuming office worker in the bustling city of Chicago. His days were filled with mundane tasks, endless meetings, and a growing overwhelming feeling. One day, while sipping his morning coffee, Eugene stumbled upon a concept: The 5-minute rule. The idea was straightforward: Whenever he encountered a task that would take less than 5 minutes to complete, he would do it immediately, without delay.

He noticed an email in his inbox, a quick response to a colleague's question. Instead of postponing it, he typed out the reply. Next, he spotted a pile of papers on his desk, invoices to file. He spent 5 minutes organizing them. Throughout the day, Eugene applied the rule to various tasks: Returning phone calls, tidying his workspace, jotting down ideas, and even stretching his legs with a short walk.

Over weeks and months, Eugene's productivity soared. The 5-minute rule became his secret weapon. He cleared the clutter, tackled minor chores, and addressed small work-related issues promptly. The cumulative effect was astonishing. Eugene felt lighter, more focused, and less overwhelmed.

Eugene Pauly's story teaches us that productivity isn't always about grand strategies or complex systems. Sometimes, small, consistent actions—the 5-minute tasks—led to remarkable results.

So, the next time you face a minor task, remember Eugene and ask yourself: "Can I tackle this in 5 minutes?" You might be surprised by the impact of such a simple rule. This may not apply to everything; if something needs more time, you give it more time. Don't tell your relatives to leave 5 minutes after they have entered your house.

Let me give you another perspective:

Guru Nanak Ji felt a deep spiritual calling to spread his message of love, equality, and devotion to God. His travels were not merely physical but also a quest for enlightenment and compassion. He primarily traveled on foot through forests, deserts, mountains, and villages.

Accompanied by his childhood friend, Bhai Mardana, who played the musical instrument Rebab, Guru Nanak Ji sang his spiritual hymns *(Shabads)* during their journey. Walking allowed them to connect with people, observe nature, and experience the challenges ordinary folks face. The journey was arduous. They encountered threats of loot, diseases, and wildlife. According to Sikh tradition, Guru Nanak Ji received divine assistance during his travels. He engaged in dialogues with scholars, saints, and ordinary folk, spreading his message of unity and love. Guru Nanak Ji's travels were fueled by his spiritual mission, determination, and divine guidance. Over a lifetime, Guru Nanak Dev Ji's extensive travels covered approximately twenty-eight thousand kilometers, which is remarkable. There have been other such saints, spiritual masters, yogis, and philosophers who have traveled across the Indian subcontinent spreading their message of spiritual wisdom and inner well-being.

The legend suggests that Agastya Muni, one of the *Saptarishis*, lived for four thousand years. However, historical accuracy cannot be verified, and some sources believe he lived around four hundred years. Regardless of the exact duration, it is clear that Agastya Muni's lifespan exceeded the norm. His immense volume of activity defies the limitations of a typical human lifespan. His accomplishments, such as extensive travel, teaching, and spiritual practices, indicate a more extended existence than usual today.

We must wonder how these yogis and rishis accomplished so much in a limited life span. Yes, they were divine entities, but they accomplished this feat in the human form. The concept of productivity did not exist during their lifetimes; however, let's see what we can learn from their divine lives to help us become more productive. If you look at the nature of life, it's a specific combination of time and energy. While we cannot control time, we can always play around with our life energies. This means if we have control over our life energies, we can accomplish much more within the same period and live many lifetimes within a single life. This is what ties up to the idea of productivity.

Productivity is a crucial ingredient for success and fulfillment in life. It allows us to maximize our time, accomplish goals, and experience satisfaction. However, in a world filled with distractions and demands, why should we give importance to productivity? Here is why:

Defining Success

Success means different things to different people. It is crucial to clarify your definition of success and align your goals and actions accordingly. While people may give a lot of different definitions to the word "success", the simplest way to define it is to design your life as per your desires. Once you have defined the core design, you need to determine what values you should teach to build that design—understanding these core values and what truly matters to you to create a foundation for productivity. Many people desire, but only a few have the courage and commitment. If we fall under the latter category, we need large chunks of time to be productive. An excellent way to judge if we are spending time productively is to do a quick dip check of our day's schedule. Baring sleep, eating food, and catering to other daily requirements like traveling, etc. We all have about ten hours of productive time in the day. Ask ourselves how much of it is fruitful and how much of that time I am using in designing my life as per my desires.

If you are already doing it, skip this chapter and move to the next one, but if you fall under the majority who struggle, read on.

Cultivating a Growth Mindset

Embrace a mindset that views challenges as opportunities for growth and learning. This mindset encourages resilience, adaptability, and continuous improvement, which are essential for maintaining productivity. If we are obsessed with becoming better every day, naturally, we will elevate towards becoming more productive. Each day, we would want to spend more time redefining our art and becoming more creative towards everyday challenges to become more productive. If we are one of those people who think that it is our company, college, teacher, manager, or parents' responsibility to make me learn, then you are facing the wrong side of the barrel. Your learning is your responsibility, period!

Prioritizing Self-Care

Productivity requires a well-nourished mind and body. Ensure we prioritize self-care by getting adequate sleep, exercising regularly, maintaining a healthy diet, and finding time for relaxation and rejuvenation. Once we have done that, productivity will become a natural subset of everything we do in whatever field of life we are in. If you need more guidance, return to the chapter on prioritizing personal health.

Revitalizing Your Life Energies

Keeping our life energies high is essential for anyone planning to do more in the given time frame. Our rishis and yogis always paid attention to the energy system of this being and channeled our life energies in the right direction.

Buddham saranam gacchami Dhammam saranam gacchami Sangham saranam Gachhami:-

I am going back to this beautiful saying, and this time, let me explain the complete meaning. It means to keep our energies high and positive; we must be in the company of the spiritual master so that their energies can rub on us. If we don't have access to this spiritual master, we must at least study and apply their teachings by reading the spiritual textbooks because their energies would flow through them. Next, if we can't do any of the above, at least be in the company of those on the spiritual path and let their energies influence us.

Productivity Hacks

- **Mind Mapping:** Mind mapping is a creative technique for organizing thoughts and ideas visually. Use it to brainstorm, plan projects, and connect concepts, enhancing productivity and fostering a deeper understanding of the subject matter. It's all about visualizing ourselves becoming more productive. Just spend 10 minutes in the day, preferably in the morning, writing down our top three priorities and how we wish to accomplish them.

- **Implementing The 5 Minute Rule:** Complete a task immediately if it takes less than five minutes as Eugene Pauly highlighted. This simple rule prevents small tasks from accumulating and helps maintain momentum throughout the day.
- **Practice the "Do Not Disturb" Principle:** Minimize distractions by turning off notifications, setting specific "focus time" blocks, and creating physical or virtual boundaries to protect your work environment. If we would like this to work in your workspace or college, let people know in advance that you will be away for this time every day or every week. Maybe put it in your Outlook calendar.
- **Single-Tasking:** Contrary to popular belief, multitasking often diminishes productivity. Instead, focus on one task at a time, give it your full attention, and complete it before moving on to the next.
- **The Pomodoro Technique:** One effective time management technique is the Pomodoro Technique, developed by Francesco Cirillo. It involves working in focused intervals of 25 minutes, followed by short breaks. This method helps maintain focus and increase productivity.
- **Eisenhower Matrix:** A productivity tool President Dwight D. Eisenhower popularized to prioritize tasks based on urgency and importance. This approach helps individuals allocate their time and energy more effectively and allows them to focus on more urgent and essential tasks.
- **Time Blocking:** Allocate specific time blocks for different

activities, such as work, personal projects, and leisure. By scheduling tasks in advance, we can eliminate decision fatigue and ensure productive use of time.

Common Mistakes

- Overcommitting to a task can cause us to become tired and disinterested. Maintain a delicate balance between productive and unproductive time.
- Outsourcing our work can often be seen as unproductive. However, it's a great tool if we can delegate or outsource smartly to focus on what we are good at.
- Always reflect upon our productive time, experiment, and see what works for us. Don't be a slave to anyone's suggestions, including mine; figure out what works for one.
- Not measuring our productivity can be counterproductive. Create small measurement scales.

Success Tip

In my book *The Great Himalayan Treasure*, I discuss the productive time matrix and the importance of ensuring that one spends at least 80% of one's time in it.

People often complain that they never seem to get anything done throughout the day, even though they seem more than busy than ever. This is because they are usually busy doing things that never add any productive element to their schedule. The best way to monitor if you are spending enough time in the productive zone is to monitor if your activity is fueling your growth engine to propel you towards achieving your life goals. If doing the activity brings you closer to your goal, please consider the time spent doing that activity productive.

Dedicate time from your everyday routine to reading books; this is the most significant difference between those who achieve and those who only dream. If books become part of your daily routine, especially early morning and late at night, you will see a remarkable change in your character and personality.

Understand that you must interact with people no matter where you go or what you do. The most productive use of your time is to develop people skills. Also, learning a new skill requires listening, asking questions, clarifying your understanding, and often reinforcing new skills in practice with others. The better you are at active listening, asking thoughtful questions of others, communicating clearly, and collaborating with team members — the more likely you'll learn faster and remember more of what you learned. Here are some of the most prolific ways that you could develop people skills:

I. Associate with people and exchange ideas with them on every possible opportunity that comes your way.

II. Listen to people with opposite thoughts to help build an overall perspective.

III. Contributing to society is the best way to acquire people skills. Selfless love is about giving your time and efforts to a cause bigger than yourself.

IV. Gratitude and kindness are the two most significant tools the human race possesses, yet they continue to be the most underutilized. People who are kind to others know their way around them.

V. People know when you're genuinely interested in them; Ryan Kahn, a career coach, puts it best. 'If you're not showing a genuine interest – asking thoughtful questions and considering their answers – your interaction can have an opposite effect to the one intended. Take care to remember names, dates, and important life events.'

VI. You must develop a natural tendency to trust others; nothing ever gets accomplished as a team unless you learn to trust people.

VII. Learn to laugh at yourself; a joyful human being is always a wonderful human being. And everyone wants to be around wonderful people. No one would ever opt to be around someone who is grumpy, frustrated, and carries a long face.

VIII. People want to work with those they know they can trust. Honesty is the foundation of any relationship, whether professional or personal. If you are not honest with the people that you are working with, it is unlikely that your relationship will last for long.

IX. Everything that comes out of your mouth should be to empower, motivate or encourage someone. Keep your criticism and complaints only restricted to yourself.

CHAPTER 18

EXPRESSION OF JOY VS PURSUIT OF HAPPINESS

NOT MANY people realize the difference between the above two words that form the heading of this chapter.

Maybe a story about a 92-year-old woman known as Peggy Jones would help. This petite, well-poised, and proud lady, who is fully dressed each morning by eight o'clock, with her hair fashionably coiffed and makeup perfectly applied, even though she is legally blind, moved to a nursing home one day. Her husband of 70 years recently passed away, making the move necessary. After many hours of waiting patiently in the nursing home lobby, she smiled sweetly when told her room was ready.

As she maneuvered her walker to the elevator, the attendant described her tiny room, including the eyelet sheets that had been hung on her window. "I love it," she stated with the enthusiasm of an eight-year-old who had just been presented with a new puppy.

"Mrs. Jones, you haven't seen the room, so just wait," said the attendant.

"That has nothing to do with it," she replied. "Happiness is something you decide on ahead of time."

"Whether I like my room or not doesn't depend on how the furniture is arranged; it's how I arrange my mind. I have already decided to love it. I make this decision every morning when I wake up. I have a choice: Spend the day in bed recounting my difficulty with the parts of my body that no longer work or get out of bed and be thankful for the ones that do.

"Each day is a gift, and as long as my eyes open, I'll focus on the new day and all the happy memories I've stored away just for this time in my life. Old age is like a bank account; you withdraw from what you've put in. So, my advice to you would be to deposit a lot of happiness in the bank account of memories," she concluded.

One of the most important decisions we make in life is deciding whether we want to be happy or unhappy; this is a conscious choice we all have. And if we are someone who thinks that this is something outside of my control, then we have already made our decision to be unhappy. It's not our family, it's not our job, it's not our friends, it's not even our dog that is in charge of our happiness; it is always us. If I could recollect a moment in my life that triggered a change in my life and rallied it in the right direction, it was when I promised myself that no matter what happens from this point onwards in my life, I would always try and be happy. Everything changed after that!

A lot of obstacles came along the way: the pain of losing my loved ones, financial difficulties, friends and family turning their back, and the struggle to find job fulfillment, but that promise kept me going.

Joy and happiness are words often used interchangeably, but there is a big difference between them. Happiness is a feeling of contentment and satisfaction, while joy is a more profound, more intense feeling. Joy is often described as peace, love, and gratitude. It is a feeling that comes from within and is not dependent on external circumstances. Happiness, on the other hand, is often more fleeting. It can be triggered by external events, such as getting a promotion, winning the lottery, or falling in love. However, happiness can also be fleeting, and it can be challenging to maintain.

Several activities can contribute to joy. Spending time with loved ones, helping others, and pursuing your passions are all activities that can lead to pleasure. Joy can also be found in the simple things in life, such as spending time in nature, listening to music, or reading a good book.

Happiness, on the other hand, is often more challenging to achieve. Good health, financial security, and strong social relationships can help. However, even if you have all of these things, it is still possible to experience periods of unhappiness. And suddenly, if they are taken away from us, our life falls apart.

I won't teach you to be joyful or give you a list of things to do to become joyful because no one can unless you choose to move to Goa.

Common Mistakes
- The young minds of today are too impatient; they want the juice even before the fruit. They want everything to happen to them now; life doesn't work like that. This breeds frustration and stress. Whether it's a relationship or a job, you must wait; it's not a sprint. Sometimes, it's a marathon.
- Never check your phone first thing in the morning. I know it's hard, but please change for good. Leave some time in the morning to settle our mind, read something that inspires, maybe do yoga, or run and wait to get in

contact with the outside world. Remember, the phone we bought is for our convenience, not for others to interfere in your life whenever they want.

- We stick around for too long, expecting people to change. It's not in your hands to change someone who doesn't want to. And if that person is creating a disturbance in your life, then it's best to move on. You would not regret this decision, indeed.
- If we are a parent, remember that we only have limited time to spend with your little bundles of joy. It will not be long before they are gone, swept away by the tides of life outside. So, the next they ask us to play with them, never say no. If we are busy doing something now, schedule some other time in the day, but make it happen. We won't regret it!
- We make a mistake when we think we don't deserve to be joyful or believe that anger is a better fuel for change. There is enough scientific evidence to suggest that we are at our best when we are joyful. Remember, the best gift we can give to ourselves, and our loved ones is to be joyful human beings.

> ## Success Tip

Whenever I feel down or frustrated, I look for something to instantly change my frequency and give me an instant dose of joy. For me, it is my daughter's laughter. Whenever I am around her, my heart automatically sings, my frustrations melt, and my frequencies become vibrant.

The idea is to explore what works for you and what your instant dose of joy is. Maybe it's sports, watching cricket, listening to music, writing, or talking to your loved ones. Figure out what that dose is and keep it aside for instant use.

CHAPTER 19

A REALIZATION THAT YOU ARE MORTAL

IN THE vibrant mosaic of Indian life stories, few are as inspiring as that of Arunima Sinha. Arunima Sinha was a national-level volleyball player with dreams of representing India on an international stage. However, her life took a dramatic turn in 2011. While traveling on a train from Lucknow to Delhi, she encountered a group of robbers who demanded her belongings. When she resisted, they threw her out of the moving train.

Arunima fell onto the adjacent tracks, and another train passed over her leg, causing severe injuries. She lay there, grievously wounded, until she was finally discovered and taken to a hospital. The medical team had no choice but to amputate her left leg below the knee to save her life.

Lying in the hospital, Arunima faced a grim reality. She had lost a limb, and with it, she feared her dreams. But it was during this period of intense physical and emotional pain that she made a pivotal decision: she would climb Mount Everest, the highest peak in the world. This decision was met with skepticism and disbelief, but Arunima was undeterred.

Arunima's recovery was a testament to her indomitable

spirit. She received a prosthetic leg and underwent rigorous physical rehabilitation. Determined to turn her life around, she began training for her monumental goal. She sought guidance from Bachendri Pal, the first Indian woman to climb Mount Everest, and trained under her mentorship.

Despite the immense physical challenges and many doubts, Arunima remained focused. Her training was grueling, involving hours of strength-building exercises, endurance training, and climbing smaller peaks to prepare herself for the ultimate challenge.

On May 21, 2013, just two years after losing her leg, Arunima Sinha reached the summit of Mount Everest. She became the first female amputee to scale the world's highest peak. Her ascent was a personal triumph and a powerful message to the world about the strength of the human spirit and the power of determination.

Arunima did not stop at Everest. She climbed several other high peaks, including Kilimanjaro in Africa, Elbrus in Europe, and Aconcagua in South America. Her achievements have earned her numerous accolades and recognition, but more importantly, they have inspired countless individuals facing their adversities.

Arunima also authored a book, *Born Again on the Mountain*, where she narrates her incredible journey and the lessons she learned. Her journey from a near-death experience to the top of the world exemplifies resilience, determination, and the ability to turn adversity into triumph. But it also demonstrates our ability to comprehend that anything can happen at any time, and we must use the available time to make something happen.

Would anyone of us want to know the day that we are going to die? Am sure not, the very thought shivers us at times. But the fact that we are going to die someday is a living reality. A reality that we try and run from, but we certainly cannot escape. But this lesson just life this book is not about death but rather about life. But it's important to know that one is not different from the other and a more profound understanding of death can propel us to live well.

A man goes to a doctor for a routine check-up. After the examination, the doctor looks at him gravely and says, "I have bad news. You only have six months to live."

The man is shocked and asks, "Isn't there anything I can do?" the doctor replies, "Well, you could try moving in with your mother-in-law."

Confused, the man asks, "Will that cure me?"

The doctor shakes his head and says, "No, but it'll make six months feel like an eternity."

The real question to ask yourself is how I can make my living experience so blissful that those eighty or ninety years of my life seem like six months. People do this the other way; their six months seem like an eternity because miserable people have long lives.

Understanding and recognizing our mortality and the limited time we have on this planet is essential to our growth as a human being and can have a transformative impact on our life. Here's why it is significant:

Embracing Impermanence: Recognizing our mortality reminds us that life is impermanent and ever-changing. Understanding this truth can help us detach from material possessions and transient desires, focusing instead on cultivating meaningful experiences and relationships. There is a beautiful story in the book *The Last Lecture* by Randy

Pausch who was a cancer patient. His lecture and subsequent book touched the hearts of millions worldwide. The story, however, goes like this: For most of his life, Pausch had no children of his own, so in his family, he was the "bachelor uncle." He revealed he was an uncle to Tammy's two children, Chris and Laura. Every month or so, he would pop into their lives and offer his unique perspective on the world. He never spoiled them but always tried to get them to see the world from "strange new angles."

When Chris was seven and Laura was nine, "Uncle Randy" picked them up in his brand-new Volkswagen convertible. Tammy warned her children not to mess up or get dirt in their uncle's new car. As Pausch listened to her admonitions, he thought these warnings set the kids up to fail; they would inevitably get the car dirty. That is what kids do. So, Pausch decided to make things easier for all of them. As Tammy recounted the many things she did not want them to do in or to his car, Pausch opened a can of soda and deliberately poured it onto the cloth seats in the back of his car. He wanted to demonstrate that people are much more important than things are. The children watched agape as their crazy uncle rejected the rules to which most adults cling.

Practicing Gratitude: The awareness of our limited time encourages us to appreciate every moment and be grateful for the blessings and opportunities we have in life. Gratitude fosters a positive mindset and enhances our overall well-being; I have mentioned this multiple times throughout this book. Like Kareena Kapoor said in Jab We Met: *"Bhai sahab, aap convince ho gaye hai ya main aur bolun?"*

Setting Priorities: Knowing life is finite prompts us to prioritize what truly matters. It allows us to align our actions and goals with our values and passions, making the most of our time. The realization of mortality thus can be a powerful motivator to stop procrastinating. It urges us to act and pursue our dreams and aspirations without delay, making the most of the present moment. If we are serious about living a life filled with unique experiences, opportunities, and wealth, we have to step away from our world of entertainment.

Deepening Spiritual Connection: Contemplating our mortality can open the door to deeper spiritual insights. It encourages us to explore questions about the purpose of life, the nature of existence, and our spiritual journey. We come closer to nature and, thus, can also cultivate compassion and empathy. When we realize that everyone, including ourselves, are on a limited journey, we may become more understanding and supportive of others.

Letting Go of Fear and being true to Yourself: Remember the story of the woman named Grace, which is mentioned in the book, *The Top Five Regrets of the Dying*. She regretted holding on to her fear for too long before she knew it was game over. Embracing the impermanence of life can help us release the fear of the unknown. Recognizing our mortality encourages us to live authentically and true to ourselves. It empowers us to genuinely express our thoughts and emotions, build authentic connections, and live a life aligned with our values.

The late Steve Jobs, co-founder of Apple Inc., famously acknowledged recognizing one's mortality. In his renowned Stanford commencement speech, he said, "Remembering that you are going to die is the best way I know to avoid the trap of thinking you have something to lose." Jobs lived his life with a sense of urgency, pursuing his passions and leaving a lasting impact on the world through his innovations. In many ways, his story ties up to Caitlin Doughty. It is not every day that you hear a professional call death a "positive advocate."

Caitlin Doughty is a mortician, author, and death positivity advocate. Doughty grew up in Kaneohe, Hawaii, where she had no exposure to death until witnessing another child fall to her death at a shopping mall when she was eight years old. This experience sparked her interest in death and its cultural significance. After moving to San Francisco, she sought hands-on exposure to modern death practices. She was hired in the crematory of Pacific Interment despite having no prior experience in the funeral industry.

Through her work, she challenges society's taboo around death and encourages open conversations about mortality. Doughty's mission is to help people embrace their mortality, have a healthier relationship with death, and make the most of their lives. She created the web series *Ask a Mortician*, which has been viewed over 200 million times. You would want to think it's inviting trouble into your life if you are constantly talking about death, but that is not true. Let's look at how some more evolved cultures looked at mortality.

Indian Culture

The intricate view of life and death can be woven through our scriptures, mythology, and everyday practices. In *Sanatan Dharma*, the concept of *Samsara* (the cycle of life, death, and rebirth) is central. Life is seen as a continuous cycle, where death is not an end but a transition to a new beginning. This belief is beautifully encapsulated in the story of Nachiketa from the Katha Upanishad.

Nachiketa was a young boy with a curious mind. One day, his father, a sage, performed a ritual where he had to give away all his possessions. However, his father was not sincere and offered only old, useless cows. Nachiketa, seeing this, asked his father, "Father, to whom will you give me?"

Angry at his son's questioning, the father rashly said, "I give you to Yama, the God of Death." Nachiketa, being obedient, went to Yama's abode. Yama was not home when he arrived, so Nachiketa waited three days without food or water. When Yama returned, impressed by the boy's patience and dedication, he offered Nachiketa three boons.

For his first boon, Nachiketa asked his father to be free from anger and welcome him back with love. For his second, he asked to learn a sacred fire ritual. For his third, he asked the most profound question: "What happens after death?"

Yama tried to dissuade him, offering wealth and a long life instead. But Nachiketa was determined. Finally, Yama, pleased with his persistence, taught him about the immortality of the soul and the cycle of rebirth.

Now, I hope you meet Yama much later in life. Either way, he is unlikely to have this life-and-death conversation with you. Therefore, I am throwing away these seeds of wisdom so you can catch some of them and sow them in your life.

Japanese Culture

Aokigahara Forest Guides: Aokigahara, also known as the "Suicide Forest," is a dense forest located at the base of Mount Fuji in Japan. However, amidst the challenges associated with the forest's reputation, some volunteers serve as guides, patrolling the area to prevent suicides and provide support to those in need. These volunteers recognize the preciousness of life and actively work to prevent tragic outcomes.

I am sure you have heard about Okinawa, Japan, a region known for its longevity; many residents embrace the concept of "ikigai" — finding purpose and meaning in life. Okinawans live with a strong sense of purpose, engaging in activities they love and maintaining strong social connections. They understand the preciousness of life and prioritize their well-being and the well-being of their community. There is a beautiful series on Netflix, *Live to 100: Secrets of the Blue Zones*. The show follows author Dan Buettner as he travels worldwide to investigate the diet, behavior, and habits of those who've lived the longest. It covers Okinawa as well as part of its endeavor. I sincerely hope you will look for content like this next time you pick up a remote and open Netflix. But it's your life, so your choice; remember, you can choose to live the way you want, but you cannot choose to live forever. The clock is ticking, Tick Tock!

Common Mistakes

- Never try to escape death because, in the pursuit of escaping death, we would escape life itself. Just the realization that death would come one day knocking down on our doors should be a realization enough that we must not waste our time on things that mean nothing to us.
- Not taking time for things we love doing; it does not need an explanation.
- Overthinking the result. What would she say, what would they think, and how would they perceive me? All this is nonsensical thinking. Just smile and go ahead; anyway, we

are at a loss if we don't try.
- Running this life like it's some race; trust me, there are no trophies to win. Savor each moment that comes our way; you never know when it will become a memory.

> ## Success Tip

Well, it's uncommon advice, but it always works. Next time you are at a crematory, do not be in a hurry to get home; spend some time understanding what's happening there. All those people who are being burned were living, walking human beings just like you and me, but now they are gone. Our problem is that we think this will not happen to us or will happen a zillion years later. No, it can happen tomorrow without us having any control over it. Our problem is that when we are there, we are thinking about our mortal nature and, as a result, thinking of making changes in our lives by always being calm and peaceful. The moment we step out, the very next minute we are fighting with the rikshaw person for ten rupees change. This lack of sincerity will not bring you anything.

CHAPTER 20

THE MOST IMPORTANT THING

AS WE near the end of this book, remember that everything above is set aside, and there is one lesson that stands tall amongst all. That's why I have kept this at the end; I was afraid you would read this one and immediately keep the book aside. Does it mean everything we have read so far is irrelevant? Certainly not. Imagine the tallest tree you would have seen; it would have come from a tiny seed you could hold in your palm. The idea of this lesson is like that little seed; if you cultivate this in your mind, heart, and soul, everything else will blossom automatically. Therefore, while the seed is where it starts for a full-fledged tree, everything is essential: the roots, the branches, the trunk, the leaves, the flowers, and the fruits.

So, let me ask you this: What is the most essential thing in life?

Is it your family that adores you? Is it the wealth you have accumulated that brings along all the material comforts? Is it the books you have read, the ones that have transformed your life? Is your community or network providing you with the social support you need? Is it your life purpose that wakes you up every morning filled with zeal and energy? Or is it the spiritual practices that keep you grounded and close to the higher being?

Stop searching for an answer elsewhere because the answer lies in the question: The most essential thing in life is life itself!

That life that thrives amongst all of us, that life that creates every experience for us. That is the most important thing.

Unfortunately, not everyone understands that. Broken after learning that he had failed in his favorite subject, Mohammad Adnan Hilal, a 17-year-old electronics engineering student, killed himself in Jammu and Kashmir in November 2015. Adnan's friends and family claimed that Physics was a subject he used to be a master of, so when he saw that he had failed, he jumped into river Jhelum. Four months after his demise, a re-evaluation of the exam paper found that he had not only passed but had also topped his class in the subject.

It's a shame we cannot create an ecosystem where our children are nurtured and protected. That's our collective karma; unfortunately, we are paying for it. But anyone reading this book must not feel the need to take this collective burden on themselves. There is no shame in seeking help and trying something else. Everything else can come back once it is gone, except our life. That is why life is referred to as the passing of time because time, too, does not come back. Now, let's talk about a full-fledged life.

What is a full-fledged life?

A full-fledged life is a life of possibilities and experiences beyond one's physical body, mental structures, and emotional bondages.

The best way to explain a full-fledged life is that there are no boundaries to your growth and no restrictions you put on yourself to explore and seek the truth.

Please understand that your life is never measured by the years you spend on this planet; it is not measured through your bank account or balance sheet numbers. No matter how much you adore social media, it is also not measured by the number of followers you have on these platforms.

If this were true, you would not follow Swami Vivekananda, who lived for only thirty-nine years, or Bhagat Singh, who passed away at the young age of twenty-three. You would certainly not follow APJ Abdul Kalam, whose only possessions at the time of his death included his books, his veena, some articles of clothing, a CD player, and a laptop. Your social media platform can create your brand, but finding a place in people's hearts requires a particular skill that only a few people possess.

So, the question is, how should one measure the scale of one's life?

Well, it is measured on two factors:
I. Intensity of Experience
II. Significance of Impact

Intensity of Experience

The more intense your experience of life is the more memories we create on our way. Just far too many people have dreams for themselves that have been borrowed from this society. Instead of spending time and energy creating more profound experiences for themselves, they start accumulating assets to show them as some trophies that they have earned. In the process of this accumulation, they forget to live their lives.

Do one thing: make a list of things that you think would enhance your experience of life. This could be those long vacations that you are planning to go, the pet which you were planning to bring home, the singing or dance lessons you were planning to attend, the public speaking competition you were planning to compete in, the small kids in the poor neighborhood you were planning to teach, the NGO you were planning to associate with, the YouTube channel you were planning to start, basically the new life you were planning to live! After you have made that list, please do yourself a favor. Just do it—not because I am telling you to but because you owe this much to yourself.

That is how I got into public speaking; the intensity of my experience was so thrilling when I was in front of people that I had to do more of it.

Significance of Impact

We must understand that the times we live in today are perhaps most conducive to the scale of impact we would like to have on this world. Never before did we have the resources to speak to the world while sitting in our bedroom, but today, it's possible, provided we have the right intentions and take appropriate actions. Thank you, YouTube!

Do note this: the right intentions aren't enough; our intentions must be backed up by action. But it would be best if we also kept in mind that every action we perform in this world directly reflects who we are. Therefore, if we want our actions to impact this world significantly, we must change our inner experience somehow.

We would have observed that those people who are naturally joyful by nature find it easier to mix in any environment, the flexibility to adapt to changes, the energy to work for longer hours, the efficiency to produce better results, the persistence to go through hardships, the focus to learn quickly, the confidence to think big and most importantly the clarity to get what they want from life.

Once this inner experience is aligned, everything we do will automatically align with our dreams. You cannot stop a person who has dissolved themself in the process; when the process becomes a person, the results become a reality.

Common Mistakes

- The young minds of today are running after everything. If we are running after two rabbits simultaneously, we might not catch either. Swami Vivekananda said, "Take up one idea. Make that one idea your life, dream of it, and live on it. Let the brain, the body, muscles, nerves, and every part of your body be full of that idea and leave every other idea alone. This is the way to success and the way great spiritual giants are produced."
- We are a complete life on your own; waiting for others to complete you is an unfulfilling prophecy. Be with someone because they love, inspire, and fulfill us, not because they complete us.
- Allowing others' opinions to become our life's facts can be fatal. Our life should be the outcome of our ideas, which we have researched and revisited repeatedly for further refinement.
- A sign of a beautiful life is that even though we may have lived for ninety years, in our experience, it is over even before it started. Far too many people engage in activities where time passes slowly, indicating that something needs to change.

Success Tip

Well, there are no success tips for life, just live to the fullest!

EPILOGUE

The old man sat on a weathered wooden bench, its paint faded and chipped over the years. The river flowed gently before him, its waters reflecting the soft hues of the setting sun. The air was filled with the soothing sounds of flowing water, birdsong, and the rustle of leaves from nearby trees.

His wrinkled hands rested on his lap, weathered, and worn like the bench beneath him. Deep lines etched across his face told tales of a life well-lived. His weathered face reflects the wisdom of years lived fully. His eyes, though aged, still sparkle with the light of cherished memories. With each passing moment, he found solace in the rhythmic flow of the water, a mirror to the passage of time. Despite the wrinkles on his face and the ache in his bones, he found contentment in the knowledge that he had lived with purpose, leaving behind a legacy of kindness and joy. With a heart full of gratitude, he watched the river carry away his worries, leaving only peace in its wake.

In the distance, the sun dipped below the horizon, casting a warm, golden glow over the landscape. The old man's thoughts were like the curving river, flowing through the bends of his past, each turn revealing cherished memories. The rhythmic babble of the river seemed to mirror the cadence of his thoughts, a steady reminder of the passage of time. As the light faded, the old man remained seated, contemplating the course of his life, and the evening draped the scene, encapsulating the old man's reflections on a lifetime filled with the wisdom of life, peace, and triumphs.

As he sits, he recalls moments from his youth, laughter shared with friends under the shade of ancient trees, the warmth of family gatherings, and the quiet beauty of starlit nights. Each memory is a treasure, a testament to a life rich in experiences and love.

The man stepped forward to touch the flowing river as he saw his reflection in the water; suddenly, his memories flashed back as he remembered coming to this place often as a child playing alongside his friends. Suddenly, his heart was filled with joy and playful energy. He recollected his youth days when his eyes were filled with dreams of a bright future filled with ecstasy and fulfillment. He reminisced about how he labored hard not just to fill his family with food but also studied harder to earn wealth, which would last many lifetimes.

He thought about his beautiful wife, who stood with him throughout his struggles and wins, always ensuring that he stayed motivated during his defeats and humble during his wins. He thought about his two children, who were now married and lived away with their families but always made time for him, for they understood the very definition of real wealth through his teachings.

Soon enough, the sun had drowned in the mountains, the breeze had stopped, and the birds had settled in their nests. It was a moment of absolute silence. The old man thought about his life and couldn't help but think about how life is always teaching us something new, something meaningful, something that could alter our lives forever, and how he had altered his life for good. You never know when the right moment will change everything; assuming every moment is right is better.

AFTER THOUGHTS

Throughout this book, we have embarked on a transformative journey together, exploring essential principles and invaluable insights that will serve as guiding stars in your life's constellation. As you stand on the precipice of adulthood, armed with newfound wisdom and understanding, let us recapitulate the critical lessons woven into this book's fabric.

As you close this book and embark on the next chapter of your life, remember that you hold the pen to your story. You are the author of your narrative, and the lessons you've internalized will serve as your compass. Embrace the uncertainties with courage, face challenges with resilience, and celebrate your victories with humility.

The path to self-discovery is not a sprint but a marathon, a journey that unfolds gradually and beautifully over time. We've learned that understanding who you are, your values, passions, strengths, and areas for growth is an ongoing process. Self-discovery requires courage to delve deep within yourself, confront your fears, and be open to change. Remember, it's okay not to have all the answers right away; life's mysteries reveal themselves gradually, like the layers of an onion.

The journey of growth and discovery does not have a final destination; it is a lifelong expedition. We've emphasized the significance of continuous learning, remaining curious, and adapting to the evolving landscape of life. Embrace change as an opportunity to learn, evolve, and uncover new dimensions of your potential.

The path ahead may not always be smooth, but armed with the insights from this book, you are equipped to navigate its twists and turns with grace and purpose. Each day presents a canvas upon which you can paint the masterpiece of your life. Be patient with yourself, trust the process, and never underestimate your capacity to learn, grow, and transform.

As your journey unfolds, may you find joy in the small moments, strength in adversity, and meaning in every experience. Embrace each lesson as a gift and remember that the journey is the destination. Congratulations, young adult, on this incredible voyage of self-discovery and growth. The world eagerly awaits the impact you will make.

A New Beginning, Not an End

This conclusion marks not the end of our exploration but the beginning of a new phase. I hope this book will remain a companion, a guide that you can return to whenever you seek wisdom, solace, or inspiration. Remember, life's lessons are not stagnant; they evolve as you do. Keep an open heart and an open mind, for the world is a classroom, and every moment offers an opportunity to learn and grow.

As you enter your life, I am grateful for allowing me to accompany you on this journey. I look forward to hearing from you about your transformation story and any feedback that would help me add more value to my readers.

With profound appreciation and warmest wishes,

Varun Wadhwa

(varunwadhwa13@gmail.com)

ACKNOWLEDGMENTS

An author is incomplete without readers, so I must start by thanking anyone and everyone who has picked up my book. Your thirst for learning is what keeps us going. There is no better way to acknowledge your contributions than by promising to continue pushing myself to improve and bring more content to life through such books.

Thank you to those wonderful souls who have supported and encouraged me to become an author. My family, friends, and loved ones, please keep the faith alive.

Sherry Bhai, thank you so much for writing the foreword for this book and for always giving people like me a platform to present their work. You are a wonderful human, and I will always be grateful for your support.

A special mention for Sagar Azad Katheria and his publishing house, Anecdote Publishing House, for always believing in me. When I met Sagar many years ago, I saw someone who was driven and had dreams of changing the landscape of the publishing industry. His team works tirelessly to create a brand for you as an author, and it feels lovely to collaborate on this project.

NOTES

Chapter 1

Information on Swami Vivekananda's and Sri Ramakrishna

https://www.ramakrishnavivekananda.info/gospel/introduction/narendra.htm

About the Book – Code of Extraordinary Mind

https://www.mindvalley.com/vishen/codex

Ray Dalio's 5 Step Process (To Getting What You Want Out Of Life)

https://commoncog.com/dalios-5-step-process-to-getting-what-you-want/

Chapter 2

Why Deepika Mhatre Considers Her Smile As A Superpower

https://www.shethepeople.tv/women-entrepreneurs/who-is-deepika-mhatre-shethepeople-40-over-40-awardee-4480634

Exclusive: This Mumbai Woman Is a Domestic Help by Day, Stand-Up Comic by Night!

https://thebetterindia.com/153761/deepika-mhatre-mumbai-domestic-help-stand-up-comedian/

Influenza pandemic of 1918–19

https://www.britannica.com/event/influenza-pandemic-of-1918-1919

"THE OBSTACLE IS THE WAY" BY RYAN HOLIDAY

https://theobstacleistheway.com/

The Causes of Sorrow And Suffering

https://www.hinduwebsite.com/sorrowseeds.asp

What is Shoonya Intensive Program?

https://isha.sadhguru.org/us/en/yoga-meditation/yoga-program-advanced/shoonya-meditation

Chapter 3

Vince Lombardi on the Hidden Power of Mastering the Fundamentals

https://jamesclear.com/vince-lombardi-fundamentals

What Oprah Knows For Sure About Her Teacher and Friend Maya Angelou

https://www.oprah.com/spirit/oprah-on-maya-angelou-what-maya-angelou-taught-oprah

What Is Classical Conditioning in Psychology?

https://www.verywellmind.com/classical-conditioning-2794859

The effect of culture on perception and cognition: A conceptual framework

https://www.sciencedirect.com/science/article/abs/pii/S0148296313001227

Four Stages of Competence: How We Learn New Skills

https://themindcollection.com/four-stages-of-competence/

Teachability Index: How Teachable are You?

https://gettingresults.com/teachability-index/

Chapter 4

18-YO Makes Friends in 43 Countries, Through Old-fashioned Letters and Post

https://www.bing.com/search?q=Rezbin+Abba%E2%80%99s&cvid=f04c24bd85434cc5b28853feadcec3e9&gs_lcrp=EgZjaHJvbWUyBggAEEUYOdIBCDE2NDRqMGo0qAIIsAIB&FORM=ANAB01&PC=ASTS

The Ultimate Guide to Stakeholder Mapping: Creating a Complete Stakeholder Map

https://projectmanagementreport.com/blog/stakeholder-map

Chapter 5

Told I Was a 'Ticking Time Bomb', I Lost 110 KG Without Drastic Diets

https://www.thebetterindia.com/292695/healthy-weight-loss-diet-daily-workout-helped-me-lose-110-kg/

From 2 Cr Salary to 2 Million Followers: How 'FoodPharmer' Started A Food Revolution in India

https://www.thebetterindia.com/350012/revant-himatsingka-food-pharmer-nutrition-ingredient-list-read-label-padhega-india-mumbai/#google_vignette

Chapter 6

Patil Kaki Shark Tank India: Founder, Story, Snacks, Sales, Deal, Valuation

https://www.geektonight.com/patil-kaki/

Can't Learn This in Business Schools': Anand Mahindra On Woman in TBI's Viral Story

https://www.thebetterindia.com/289363/anand-mahindra-praises-patil-kaki-maharashtrian-food-business-in-viral-tweet/#google_vignette

A Guide to Money Consciousness for creating Abundance

https://intentionaleblog.com/money-consciousness/

Chapter 7

The Stanford Prison Experiment

https://www.verywellmind.com/the-stanford-prison-experiment-2794995

Bill Gates tells Harvard students how he overcame his fears to make Microsoft a success

https://finance.yahoo.com/news/bill-gates-tells-harvard-students-160100713.html

Buddham Saranam Gacchami Chant: Complete Lyrics & Meaning

https://www.insightstate.com/spirituality/buddham-saranam-gacchami/

Chapter 8

Verghese Kurien: Know all about the man and the movement on World Milk Day

https://www.hindustantimes.com/india-news/verghese-kurien-know-all-about-the-man-and-the-movement-on-world-milk-day-101622538471943.html

Verghese Kurien's Legacy: Transforming India's Dairy Sector and Challenges Ahead

https://medium.com/@adhithya1199/verghese-kuriens-legacy-transforming-india-s-dairy-sector-and-challenges-aheaddcea3e327dc7

Companies That Failed to Innovate and Went Bankrupt

https://www.investopedia.com/articles/investing/072115/companies-went-bankrupt-innovation-lag.asp

Chapter 9

7 Stories from Swami Vivekananda's Life

https://isha.sadhguru.org/en/wisdom/article/stories-swami-vivekananda-life-inspired

The Four Paths of Yoga: Karma, Jnana, Bhakti and Raja Yoga Explained

https://www.fitsri.com/articles/4-paths-of-yoga

Chapter 10

Harry Miller: Ohio State offensive lineman says he is medically retiring from football, citing mental health struggles

https://edition.cnn.com/2022/03/11/sport/ohio-state-harry-miller-medically-retiring-spt-intl/index.html

Suicide rates among young people continue to rise, but there are ways to help

https://www.uclahealth.org/news/suicide-rate-highest-among-teens-and-young-adults

The NCRB Suicide in India 2022 Report: Key Time Trends and Implications

https://journals.sagepub.com/doi/full/10.1177/02537176241240699

Chapter 11

From 2 Cr Salary to 2 Million Followers: How 'FoodPharmer' Started A Food Revolution in India https://www.thebetterindia.com/350012/revant-himatsingka-food-pharmer-nutrition-ingredient-list-read-label-padhega-india-mumbai/#google_vignette

High-Salary Career Options for Economists

https://inomics.com/advice/high-salary-career-options-for-economists-1476133

Sports and Child Development

https://www.ncbi.nlm.nih.gov/pmc/articles/PMC4856309/

Benefits of Sports for Students

https://www.jbcnschool.edu.in/blog/benefits-sports-students/#:~:text=Several%20studies%20suggest%20playing%20sports,players%20raise%20the%20self%2Desteem.

Charles de Vaulx, IVA's noted value investor, found dead at New York offices

https://www.reuters.com/article/idUSL1N2MK38H/

Chapter 12

The chapter is a summarized version of my first book: *'Books, Ideas & You.'*

Chapter 13

Tools and Weapons

https://www.penguinrandomhouse.com/books/604709/tools-and-weapons-by-brad-smith-and-carol-ann-browne/

How a 60-YO Grandmom Became a YouTube Star & Global Sensation With Millions of Fans

https://thebetterindia.com/277860/youtube-star-milkuri-gangavva-life-story-the-village-show-million-fans-viral/

10 Golden Rules Of Personal Branding

https://www.forbes.com/sites/goldiechan/2018/11/08/10-golden-rules-personal-branding/

Chapter 14

The boy who complained about everything

https://kidsofintegrity.com/activity/gratitude/boy-who-complained-about-everything/

Want to Relieve Stress ASAP? Write in a Gratitude Journal

https://www.verywellmind.com/writing-in-a-gratitude-journal-for-stress-relief-3144887

Chapter 15

Karambir Kang: Man with steely spirit, a 26/11 hero who fought with no guns

https://www.timesnownews.com/india/article/mumbai-terror-attack-2008-karambir-kang-taj-mahal-hotel-general-manager-wife-children-exemplary-courage-hero/519473

Rohit Deshpande

https://www.hbs.edu/faculty/Pages/profile.aspx?facId=6447

The Ordinary Heroes of the Taj

https://hbr.org/2011/12/the-ordinary-heroes-of-the-taj

Adam Grant

https://adamgrant.net/book/give-and-take/

Chapter 17

The Udasis of Guru Nanak Dev Ji

https://www.dhansikhi.com/the-udasis-of-guru-nanak-dev-ji/

Agastya Muni - The Father of Southern Indian Mysticism

https://isha.sadhguru.org/en/wisdom/article/agastya-muni-father-southern-india-mysticism

21 Productivity Tips, Hacks, & Strategies For Maximum Focus

https://www.scienceofpeople.com/productivity-tips/

Chapter 19

This inspiring story of the first female amputee to climb Mount Everest will make you proud

https://www.indiatoday.in/lifestyle/people/story/arunima-sinha-inspiring-story-first-indian-female-amputee-mount-everest-proud-mountain-climb-lifest-14272-2016-06-15

Randy Pausch's Last Lecture

https://www.cmu.edu/randyslecture/

Regrets of the Dying

https://bronnieware.com/blog/regrets-of-the-dying/

Caitlin Doughty

https://caitlindoughty.com/

The Story of Nachiketa - Intensity on the Spiritual Path

https://isha.sadhguru.org/en/wisdom/article/nachiketa-story

Why is Japan's Aokigahara Forest Called the 'Suicide Forest'?

https://history.howstuffworks.com/world-history/suicide-forest.htm

Want to live a long, healthy life? 6 secrets from Japan's oldest people

https://www.weforum.org/agenda/2021/09/japan-okinawa-secret-to-longevity-good-health/

Chapter 20

Four Months After This J&K Student Committed Suicide For Failing, Re-evaluation Shows He'd Topped His Class!

https://www.indiatimes.com/news/india/four-months-after-this-j-k-student-committed-suicide-for-failing-re-evaluation-shows-he-d-topped-his-class-247275.html